from my   to your
HEART ♥ KITCHEN

from my HEART ♥ KITCHEN to your

family friends & the food we ♥ to eat

Laura Laird

Tate Publishing & Enterprises

Published by Tate Publishing & Enterprises, LLC
127 E. Trade Center Terrace | Mustang, Oklahoma 73064 USA
1.888.361.9473 | www.tatepublishing.com

Tate Publishing is committed to excellence in the publishing industry. The company reflects the philosophy established by the founders, based on Psalm 68:11,
"The Lord gave the word and great was the company of those who published it."

Book design copyright © 2011 by Tate Publishing, LLC. All rights reserved.
Cover design by Kristen Verser
Interior design by Stephanie Woloszyn

Published in the United States of America

ISBN: 978-1-61739-576-5
Cooking / General
11.01.17

Dedication

I want to dedicate this book to my husband, Ken, and my two daughters, Faith and Grace. Ken, thank you for your encouragement and support throughout the whole writing process. Having you as my sounding board was so wonderful because it helped me "sound out" the book as I was writing it, which made the whole process so much easier. Faith and Grace, I think that every child wants to know about their parent's past at some point in their lives. Someday, this book will be an insight for you into how I lived as a child. My life was very different than your own, so the stories I wrote here will open your eyes to other ways of life for people born in a different culture.

Acknowledgments

First, I want to thank God for giving me the idea for this book and for literally helping me every step of the way. I started many books, but for some reason I was never able to finish them until now. From the day God dropped the idea in my heart for the kind of book I should write to the last word on the last page, He guided me through the whole process. I believe this was the only reason why I was able to write it in a week without even a hint of "writer's block" on the way.

To my husband, Ken, over our almost fourteen years of marriage, I had many ideas of things I could do, businesses I could start, books I could write. Some of those ideas were a little far-fetched even for me, and yet through it all you supported me! It was the same with this book. Without your constant support and encouragement, I would not have even started it, and that's not all! The fact is you are the reason why I am so bold in taking risks and embracing change because you help me believe in myself and believe that I can do everything I put my mind to! For all you are and all you do, thank you! And with all my heart, I love you!

To my friends, Mary-Evelyn and Alicia, thank you for cheering me on and for allowing me to test new recipes on you and your families! I am grateful that you have always embraced my culture and encouraged me to express it, especially through my cooking.

Table of Contents

69 SECTION 2

Endless Possibilities: My Eclectic Style and Falling in Love with Food All over Again

Acknowledgments

First, I want to thank God for giving me the idea for this book and for literally helping me every step of the way. I started many books, but for some reason I was never able to finish them until now. From the day God dropped the idea in my heart for the kind of book I should write to the last word on the last page, He guided me through the whole process. I believe this was the only reason why I was able to write it in a week without even a hint of "writer's block" on the way.

To my husband, Ken, over our almost fourteen years of marriage, I had many ideas of things I could do, businesses I could start, books I could write. Some of those ideas were a little far-fetched even for me, and yet through it all you supported me! It was the same with this book. Without your constant support and encouragement, I would not have even started it, and that's not all! The fact is you are the reason why I am so bold in taking risks and embracing change because you help me believe in myself and believe that I can do everything I put my mind to! For all you are and all you do, thank you! And with all my heart, I love you!

To my friends, Mary-Evelyn and Alicia, thank you for cheering me on and for allowing me to test new recipes on you and your families! I am grateful that you have always embraced my culture and encouraged me to express it, especially through my cooking.

Table of Contents

69 SECTION 2

Endless Possibilities: My Eclectic Style and Falling in Love with Food All over Again

211 SECTION 3
I Love the Holidays: Easter, Thanksgiving, and Christmas

SECTION 4

Let's End It on a Sweet Note: A Few Recipes for Your "Sweet Tooth"

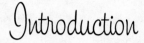

Introduction

The Lord is my Shepherd, I shall not want...
Psalm 23:1

The book you are about to enjoy is a journey through parts and events in my life that are significant to me. Looking back, even though I was not a Christian for the first twenty-five years of my life, I truly believe God was watching over me.

To begin with, I wasn't even supposed to be born, and at the age of three, I became sick with a particularly hard strain of bronchitis, which eventually became bronchial asthma. Through out my life, I had quite a few "close calls" concerning my health, since I lived in a country where the doctors were great, friendly, and knowledgeable, but the resources left a lot to be desired.

I understand now as I step into my forties that God had a plan, and I am grateful that He helped me and guided me even when I didn't know Him, through hard times, through happy times, leading me here where I am today. I often tell people that I don't regret the hardships I had in my life because through each one I learned something valuable that helped me change for the better. When I first became a Christian, I learned that God knows all the days of our life! Everything we have done, we do, and we will do, our past, present, and future, nothing is hidden from Him. This, I think, is a source of angst for people who don't believe because they consider a life lived that way dull and uneventful. After all, how can you be spontaneous, make mistakes, grow and learn if someone has already written the beginning, middle, and end of your life?

I actually think living this way is the best of both worlds. God will not tell you everything that is to happen, and He will not make your decisions for you. You still get to choose and make mistakes, learn and grow, but there is a powerful sense of security that comes with knowing that no matter what scrapes you might get into, the maker of the universe is there to back you up! I believe God gives all of us gifts, and I thank Him for choosing to give me the gift of cooking because I believe this is one of those gifts that is at the core of one of the things He loves most: family and friends! There's nothing better for me than to cook a tasty meal and eat it with my family and my friends over a glass of wine, laughing, sharing stories, and fellowshipping together. There is a scripture I love that says that where love is, God abides. To me, love is sitting right at the table when we gather like that, so God must be there enjoying it too. The more I read and learn about the different cuisines that different countries have, the more I believe food is universal.

Since I've moved here, I've watched many cooking shows, read many cookbooks, and sampled many different dishes. I have enjoyed them all, but I have noticed that a lot of ingredients, methods of cooking, and techniques are common to all the dishes. I believe that is because cooking is mostly learned from generation to generation and recipes are passed on from grandmother, to mother, to daughter, etc. Some recipes may have different names in different countries but the basic ingredients and method of cooking are the same. But no matter who is cooking or where the recipe comes from, there is something beautiful and fulfilling about tasting something delicious you made yourself, sharing that food with friends and family, and making them smile. My desire is that this cookbook will not just give you recipes, but will bring you satisfaction through trying new things and make your gatherings with friends and family happier and more unforgettable. From my heart to your kitchen, with love.

SECTION 1

Family, Friends, & Especially Food:
Growing Up in a Different World

Yeah, We Use an Outhouse, but Look at This Food

When I was growing up in Romania, food was sparse especially in the smaller cities and rural areas. Things were a little better in the capital and in major cities, but in general, a lot of people had to do with very little. But as we all know, necessity is the mother of invention, so a lot of people got very creative with food by stretching what they had and finding new uses for the same ingredients. In rural areas especially, people grew their own vegetables, raised animals, and farmed crops. All of us canned vegetables and fruits in the summer, and we also ate lots of rice, beans, and potatoes.

My paternal grandparents lived in a small village called Valea Calugareasca. They had electricity, but no running water and no bathrooms. Yes, you guessed it! They had an outhouse! I have to admit, that part was never fun when I stayed with them. They cooked on a wood-burning stove and brought in water from a common well used by many of the families in the village. Their home was heated by large, floor-to-ceiling, wood-burning terracotta stoves placed in two rooms in the house. They had a garden where they grew tomatoes, green onions, green garlic, and strawberries. They also had plum and cherry trees, a small vineyard, and about a one-half acre field where they grew corn. They made wine, and they used the corn to make corn meal and to feed their chickens and turkeys. Some years they raised pigs and sometime even goats. I spent many summer breaks there working with my grandmother in the field and learning to cook. My grandmother made many yummy things, but one of the meals I remember most was very simple but so very delicious. Roast chicken with polenta and garlic sauce. I remember sitting outside around a large and very old wooden table under a big porch with my parents, aunt and uncle, my cousins, and my grandparents eating, laughing, and having a great time. We made our own fun and entertainment, and most of it was with family and friends around food. Here is my version of those recipes.

Oven-Roasted Lemon Chicken

1 3.5 to 4 lb whole chicken
1 whole lemon, quartered plus 3 to 4 slices
1 tbsp minced fresh parsley
1 tbsp minced fresh dill
2 fresh garlic cloves, grated
½ stick butter softened
½ stick butter, melted
1 tbsp lemon juice
2 tsp lemon zest
3 to 4 tbsp olive oil
Salt and pepper

Preheat oven to 400 degrees F. Remove the giblets from the cavity and pat the outside and inside of the chicken dry with paper towels. Season the cavity with salt and pepper. In a medium bowl mix the softened butter with the minced parsley and dill, the grated garlic and 1 tsp each salt and pepper until it becomes a soft paste. Use your fingers to very gently lift the skin from the chicken breast. Make sure not to puncture the skin. Using your hand spread the butter paste all over the chicken breast under the skin. Place the lemon slices over the paste then replace the skin. Cut the whole lemon in 4 pieces and place it inside the cavity of the chicken. Tie the legs together with kitchen string and

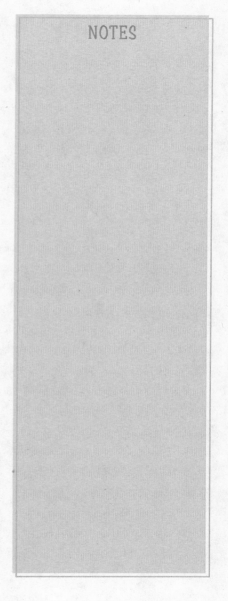

NOTES

21

NOTES

tuck the wings under the body of the chicken. Mix the melted butter, olive oil, lemon zest and juice well. Liberally season the outside of the chicken with salt and pepper, brush the outside of the chicken with some of the olive oil and butter mixture then sprinkle again lightly with salt. Place the chicken in a roasting pan with a rack and roast in the preheated 400-degree oven for 15 minutes. Turn the temperature down to 375 degrees and continue roasting until an instant thermometer inserted in the thickest part of the thigh reads between 165 to 170 degrees. Allow about 17 to 20 minutes per pound. Towards the end of the cooking time, brush the skin with the remaining melted butter, olive oil, lemon zest and lemon juice mixture about 3 times. Remove from the oven and allow the chicken to rest at least 10 minutes before carving. Reserve any pan juices for the garlic sauce. Enjoy!

Polenta with Cheese and Fresh Herbs

1 ½ cups yellow corn meal

3 cups chicken broth

2 cups milk

½ cup freshly grated Parmesan cheese

½ cup freshly grated Pecorino Romano cheese

1 tbsp butter

1 tbsp olive oil

½ cup minced fresh parsley

½ cup finely chopped fresh basil

Salt and pepper to taste

In a heavy saucepan, bring the chicken broth, milk, and 1 tablespoon olive oil to a boil. Season with salt, turn the heat down to med-low, and gradually stir in the corn meal a little at the time, mixing continually. Turn the heat down to low, and simmer the polenta until thickened, stirring frequently, about 15 to 20 minutes. Remove from the heat, and add 1 tablespoon butter and all the cheese, and mix to incorporate. Add the fresh herbs and more salt and pepper if necessary. Serve hot with the chicken.

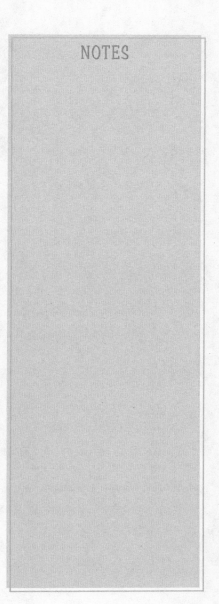

NOTES

NOTES

Garlic Sauce

2 tbsp butter
1 tbsp olive oil
4 large garlic cloves, minced
2 large garlic cloves, grated
1 cup chicken broth, warm
Pan drippings from the roast chicken
2 tbsp minced fresh parsley

In a small saucepan, heat up the butter and olive oil on medium heat until hot but not smoking. Add the minced garlic, and cook, mixing often, for about 2 minutes. Make sure not to burn the garlic. Add the pan drippings, mix, and cook together for about 1 minute. Add the chicken broth and bring to a boil. Remove from the heat, add the grated garlic, fresh parsley, and season with salt and pepper to taste. Serve hot over the chicken and polenta or use to dunk the chicken before you eat it.

It's Always Better at Grandma's House

My maternal grandmother also loved to cook, and gatherings at her house were many. From special occasions, like birthdays or anniversaries, to simple, spontaneous visits, she always had something special to give us. One of her signature dishes was oven-baked chicken legs quarters with carrots and zucchini rice pilaf, which in our part of the world is any rice cooked until very soft and creamy instead of *al dente*. She made many things, but this particular dish always made my mouth water. Actually, I learned from her when I was about six years old that it is best to sauté the rice in oil before adding the hot liquid and cooking it slowly on low heat. In Romania, already prepared chicken broth was not available and we didn't always have extra chicken to make our own broth, so we usually cooked rice in water seasoned with salt, pepper, and various dried herbs. I loved sitting in my grandmother's tiny kitchen listening to stories about her life as a young woman and learning how to cook. We had a very special relationship, which I still cherish even though she is no longer with us. She lived through war, famine, poverty, and all kinds of hardships, and yet she kept her sense of humor and a very positive attitude throughout her whole life. Her and my grandfather were married for over fifty years, and theirs was a true love story. I found a picture of the two of them once. On the back, my grandfather had written, "sitting next to the woman I will love for the rest of my life." That picture and his words are a memory that will forever be imprinted on my heart. Here's my version of that mouth-watering meal made a little better for you with brown rice.

25

NOTES

Oven-Baked Garlic Chicken Legs Quarters

4 chicken leg quarters
4 tbsp butter, softened
4 tbsp olive oil
8 large fresh garlic cloves, grated
2 tbsp dried parsley
1 tbsp-dried dill
1 tbsp + 1 tsp granulated garlic
½ tsp cayenne pepper
Salt and pepper to taste

Preheat oven to 375 degrees. Pat the leg quarters dry with paper towels. In a bowl, mix together the olive oil, grated garlic, dried herbs, and cayenne pepper until it forms a paste. Season with salt and pepper, divide the paste into 4 equal parts, and set aside. Using your fingers, gently lift the skin from the chicken thighs, being careful not to remove it completely or puncture the skin. Rub each thigh with some of the garlic and olive oil paste. Replace the skin, and season the leg quarters with salt and pepper. Mix the granulated garlic with 1 tbsp dried parsley. Rub each leg quarter with about ½ tablespoon of softened butter; then season with the granulated garlic and parsley mixture. Sprinkle again with a little salt. Place in the preheated oven and bake for about 30 to 45 minutes until an instant thermometer inserted in the thickest part of the leg reads 160 degrees. The olive oil and garlic paste will season and baste the legs from the inside out, and the butter rub will make the skin crisp and golden brown. Remove from the oven, and let the leg quarters rest, covered for a few minutes before serving.

NOTES

NOTES

Carrots and Zucchini Rice Pilaf

2 cups brown rice

6 cups chicken broth, heated

4 tbsp olive oil

2 tbsp butter

1 tbsp-dried parsley

1 tbsp-dried basil

1 small red onion, finely diced

2 large carrots, finely diced

3 medium to large zucchini, finely diced

¼ cup cream or half and half

Juice of ½ small lemon

2 tbsp minced fresh parsley

1 tbsp minced fresh basil

1 garlic clove, grated

Salt and pepper to taste

In a medium saucepan that has a fitted lid, heat 2 tablespoons of olive oil and 1 tablespoon butter on medium heat until hot but not smoking. Add the red onion and carrots, and cook for about 5 minutes, until softened. Add the zucchini, and cook for another 2 minutes. Add the rice, and cook together for about 5 minutes, mixing often. Turn the heat to high, add the warm chicken broth, 2 tablespoons of olive oil, dried parsley, and basil. Season with salt and pepper to taste, mix together, and bring to a boil. Cover, turn the heat down to low, and cook until the rice has absorbed all the liquid and it's very soft. Remove from the heat, add 1 tablespoon butter, the cream, lemon juice, fresh herbs, and grated garlic clove, and mix gently with a fork to keep the rice fluffy and airy. Check for salt and pepper, and serve hot with the chicken leg quarters.

NOTES

There Is No Place Like Home

One of my favorite memories growing up is when I would come home on winter nights and my mother was cooking. The kitchen was warm, and I could smell the wonderful aromas before I came in the door. Because we could not get any pre-prepared, ready-made, or fast food, and restaurants were few and expensive, we had to make everything we wanted to eat from scratch. In the summer, it was a little easier because we had a street market where people from the neighboring villages came and sold their fresh produce so our meals were more varied and easier to put together. But in the late fall, winter, and early spring months, we cooked with what we preserved and canned ourselves during summer. The only things we could buy from the store in those months were beans, potatoes, and sometimes some meat from the meat markets; usually, though, we could only get beef or pork bones and chicken wings in small bags. Because of this, my mother would cook only once a week during those months, on Saturday or Sunday, and she would make two big pots—usually one with some kind of soup and one with some kind of stew. All week we ate those two staples, adding maybe some polenta, beans, or, on rare occasions, pasta to complete the meal. It may sound different, but we were used to it, and whatever my mother made was delicious. I started cooking by her side when I was twelve years old, and the first thing I made was a sort of dumpling soup. The broth was not bad, but the dumplings were awful! They were so heavy and hard they were almost inedible, but my parents ate them anyway. My mother encouraged me to not give up and continue trying. Soon I fell in love with cooking, coming up with recipe ideas and watching my parents enjoy the results. Because of the reasons I mentioned earlier, everyone had to learn to cook in order to have something to eat, but not everyone enjoyed cooking. I did! Today cooking has become a passion, a way of expressing myself, and the biggest reward I get is making people happy with my food! Here are two of those recipes I learned at my mother's side.

Chicken Soup with Fresh Herbs and Grits Dumplings

❤ Soup ❤

1 rotisserie chicken, cooled, meat removed, and cut into small cubes

1 white or yellow onion, diced

1 leek, white and light green parts only, finely chopped

6 fresh garlic cloves, minced

1 small white cabbage, very finely chopped

1 cup chopped fresh spinach

1 cup frozen corn kernels, defrosted

1 bunch chopped fresh parsley

1 bunch chopped fresh dill

1½ to 2 quarts chicken broth, heated

4 tbsp olive oil

2 tbsp butter

¼ cup cream or half and half

2 tbsp lemon juice

Salt and pepper to taste

Preheat oven to 400 degrees. Spread the corn on a sheet pan, sprinkle with salt and 2 tablespoons of olive oil, and mix to coat. Roast the corn for 15 to 20 minutes until

33

NOTES

golden brown. Remove and set aside. In the meantime, place a large, heavy Dutch oven on medium to high heat. Add 2 tablespoons of olive oil and 1 tablespoon of butter, and heat until hot but not smoking. Add the onions and leeks, and sauté for about 5 minutes until softened. Add the garlic, and cook for another minute. Season with salt and pepper to taste, then add the chicken pieces and cook together for a couple of minutes. Add 1 quart warm chicken broth, bring to a boil on medium to high heat, reduce the heat, and let the soup simmer for about 5 minutes on low to medium heat. Add the corn and cabbage and ½ or 1 additional quart of chicken broth, depending on how much liquid you prefer in your soup. Simmer for an additional 5 minutes. Add the chopped spinach and mix in. At this point, turn the heat to low, and start adding the dumplings to the simmering soup. At the end when the soup and dumplings are done, add the cream and fresh herbs and simmer for just a minute. Remove from heat, add the lemon juice, and mix gently. Cover and let it rest for 5 minutes. Serve hot.

❤ Dumplings ❤

1 cup grits
2 eggs
1 tbsp chicken broth or water
Salt

Separate the yolks from the whites. Mix the egg yolks with the grits, chicken broth (or water) and salt to taste until they become pale and the mixture is well incorporated. In a separate bowl, beat the egg whites until they form soft peaks. Very gently fold the egg whites into the grits and yolk mixture with a spatula until incorporated. Using a tablespoon, drop the mixture into the already simmering soup, one tablespoon at a time until all the mixture is gone. Have a small bowl with water nearby, and dip the tablespoon in the water after each time so that the mixture does not stick to the spoon and it falls easily into the soup. Let the dumplings simmer for 5 minutes. Add ¼ cup of cold water to the soup, turn the heat to med-high, and let it simmer for another 5 minutes. Repeat the process once more with another ¼ cup of cold water, and simmer for an additional 5 minutes. Finish as shown in the soup recipe. Remove from the heat and serve. Adding the cold water will make the dumplings soft and light.

NOTES

From the author:

Do not start making the dumplings until the soup is almost ready.

NOTES

From the author:

You can find ready packaged, cut beef bones in almost any supermarket. Also, you can substitute beef bones for pork or lamb bones, or you can use a mixture.

Beef Bones Soup with Tomatoes

2 to 3 lbs beef bones

2 cups rib-eye steak, pan grilled to rare and cubed

2 large red onions, coarsely chopped

2 leeks, white and light green parts only, coarsely chopped

8 garlic cloves, minced

1 turnip, peeled and cubed

2 large carrots, peeled and cubed

2 large parsnips, peeled and cubed

6 to 8 medium-sized Yukon gold potatoes, cubed

1 bunch celery, ends cut and coarsely chopped

2 ½ to 3 quarts beef broth, heated

1 tsp beef bullion

1 bag frozen pearl onions

1 bag frozen pees

2 cans diced tomatoes

2 tbsp tomato paste

1 bunch kale, stems removed and chopped

2 cups chopped fresh spinach

¼ cup cream, warm

¼ cup red wine vinegar

2 tbsp fresh lemon juice

1 cup chopped fresh parsley

½ cup chopped fresh cilantro

Rinse the beef bones with cold water, and add them to a large soup pot. Cover with cold water, and place it on high heat. Bring to a boil, turn down the heat, and simmer until the liquid reduces by half. Strain the liquid, discard the bones, and set aside. In the same soup pot set on medium to high heat, add 3 tablespoons of olive oil and 1 tablespoon of butter, and heat until hot but not smoking. Add the onions, leeks, celery, and carrots, season with salt and pepper, and sauté until slightly softened for about 5 minutes. Add the minced garlic, and sauté for 1 minute. Add the cooking liquid, 2 quarts beef broth, and 1-teaspoon beef bullion, season again, and bring to a boil. Set the heat to medium-low, add the parsnips and turnip, and simmer for 5 minutes. Add the potatoes, and simmer for 2 minutes; then add the pees and pearl onions, and simmer for another 5 minutes. In the meantime, thin the tomato paste with a little water, and add it to the soup along with the diced tomatoes, kale, and the rib-eye steak. At this point, if needed, add more of the warm beef broth. Simmer for 5 to 7 minutes. Add the spinach and cream, and simmer for an additional 7 to 10 minutes. Remove from the heat; add the vinegar, lemon juice, parsley, and cilantro; check for seasoning, mix well, cover, and let it rest for about 5 minutes. Serve hot!

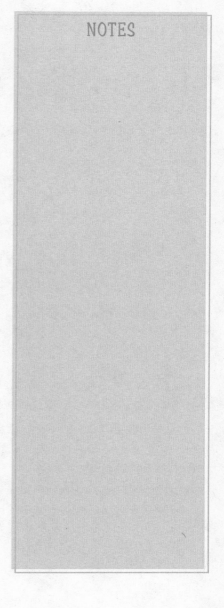

NOTES

You Want Me to Eat What?

In my country, nothing was really in abundance. People stood in very long lines for many hours for fresh bread, any kind of meat, or dairy products and eggs, and many times left the line without anything because the store ran out before everybody could buy something. For many years, flour, sugar and oil were rationed, and many of us rarely ate things like sour cream and butter. Even things like hard salami or deli cheese were sparse and sometimes non-existent. I was eighteen years old when I drank my first Pepsi, and I ate things like bananas and oranges only once a year during the Christmas holidays and sometimes not even then. One year the store had mandarins, and I thought I had died and gone to heaven when I tasted my first one! I think I was about ten years old that year. I didn't even know things like olive oil or avocados existed until I came to America. Because of all this, when we did have a chance to eat beef or pork, we actually cooked and ate just about everything from the animal except the hooves. Well, the cow hooves, anyway, because we did cook pigs' feet as well as the pigs' ears and snout! Actually one of my favorite things to eat during the Christmas holidays growing up was the Romanian version of headcheese, which we called "piftie." Things like beef tongue, heart, kidneys, liver, or even lungs, which we mostly cooked on the grill, were a delicacy for us, and I thoroughly enjoyed eating all of them. I have encountered many people here that baulk at the very idea of eating things like pig's feet, ears, or snout or organs, especially liver or kidneys, but for those of you daring few out there, here's my version of two of my favorite recipes growing up.

Headcheese

1 to 2 lb pork ears and snout, cleaned and cut in
   medium chunks

2 pigs feet

1 lb lean pork such as loin chops, some bone in, cut
   in chunks

2 quarts (8 cups) chicken broth, heated

12 garlic cloves minced

1 tbsp peppercorns

2 bay leaves

1 bouquet garnis (fresh parsley, dill, and thyme sprigs
   bundled together with kitchen string)

Salt and pepper to taste

Olive oil

8 or 10 medium-sized shallow ramekins

Heat 4 tablespoons of olive oil in a large stockpot until
hot but not smoking. Add the pork loin pieces and pork
ears and snout, and cook until starting to brown. Add the
pig's feet, heated chicken broth, peppercorns, bay leaves,
and bouquet garni season with salt and pepper, bring to
a boil, lower heat and simmer, uncovered, until the liquid
has reduced by half. Remove from the heat, and take out
the meat, bay leaves, and bouquet garni. Add the minced
garlic, cover, and let it sit undisturbed for 10 to 15 minutes.

NOTES

From the author:

We served this dish as an
appetizer over Christmas holidays.
If you cannot find pork snout, you
can use ears only

NOTES

In the meantime, chop the loin meat, the meat from the pig's feet, and the pig's ears. After the 10 to 15 minutes, strain the broth, skim some of the fat from the top, and let it cool for a few minutes. In the meantime, place equal amounts of the chopped meat in the bottom of each ramekin. When the broth is cooled, using a small strainer, fill each ramekin with some of the broth. Refrigerate the ramekins until the broth has the consistency of hardened gelatin. For a different take on this dish, chop 2 carrots and 2 zucchinis in small cubes, dice 1 small onion, and sauté all vegetables in some butter. Add 1 cup white wine, season with salt and pepper, and cook until all the wine has evaporated. Add some of the sautéed vegetables to the ramekins along with the meat before adding the broth.

Beef Tongue with Olives

1 beef tongue

1 lb black or kalamata olives

1 large red onion, finely chopped

4 to 6 large fresh garlic cloves, minced

1 bunch celery, ends removed, chopped

1 large green bell pepper, chopped

1 cup chopped fresh spinach

1 tbsp tomato paste

1 tbsp flour

2 tbsp butter, 1 softened

1 cup white wine, room temperature

1 cup cooking liquid, warm or room temperature

2 bay leaves

2 celery ribs cut in half

½ red onion cut in half

¼ cup cream, warm

½ cup minced fresh parsley

¼ tsp cayenne pepper

1 tbsp lemon juice

Olive oil

Salt and pepper

Place the beef tongue in a large pot, and cover with cold water. Add 1 bay leaf, 2 celery ribs, 2 onion quarters, and

> ### NOTES
>
> **From the author:**
>
> Beef tongue needs about 1 hour per pound to cook.

43

NOTES

bring to a boil. Add 1 to 2 tablespoons salt, reduce the heat, cover, and simmer for 1 hour per pound. Remove from the pot, and let it cool. Strain the cooking liquid and reserve 1 cup. When the tongue is cooled, remove the roots, if any, and peel off the outer skin, which should come off very easily. Slice the tongue in half long ways, then slice in ½-inch pieces. Set aside covered. In a large saucepan or Dutch oven, heat 2 tablespoons of olive oil and 1 tablespoon of butter on medium heat until hot but not smoking. Add the onions, celery, and bell pepper, season with salt and pepper and sauté until softened for about 5 minutes. Add the minced garlic, and cook for 1 minute. Add the tomato paste, and mix well. Add the olives, wine, cooking liquid, cayenne pepper, salt, and pepper, and 1 bay leaf, and bring to a boil. Reduce the heat, and simmer until the liquid reduces by half. In a small bowl, mix the softened tablespoon of butter with 1 tablespoon of flour, and add it to the sauce. Mix well until it starts to thicken. Gently mix in the warm cream, and simmer for about 2 minutes. Add the spinach, and simmer for another 2 minutes. Add the cooked, sliced tongue, mix in, cover and simmer for 5 minutes at very low heat. Remove from the heat; add the fresh parsley and lemon juice. Mix and serve hot.

This recipe can be served over rice, potatoes, quinoa, pasta, or anything you might prefer. My favorite way is served over sour-cream-and-herbs mashed potatoes. Here's my recipe:

Sour-Cream-and-Herbs Mashed Potatoes

10 to 12 medium size new red potatoes, skin on

2 tbsp butter

½ cup half-and-half or whole milk

2 tbsp sour cream

½ cup freshly grated Parmesan cheese

2 tbsp minced fresh parsley

2 tbsp minced fresh dill

1 garlic clove, grated

Salt and pepper ·

Wash and cut the potatoes in quarters. Place in a medium-sized, tall pot, and cover with cold water. Place the pot on high heat, and bring to a boil. Add 1 tablespoon of salt, and continue boiling until the potatoes are very tender, for about 20 minutes. Strain and place the potatoes back in the pot. In the meantime, add the butter and half-and-half or milk to a small saucepan, and bring to a boil. Remove and set aside. Mash the potatoes well; mix in enough of the hot milk and butter to make the potatoes soft but still stiff. It could take all the liquid, depending on how many potatoes you used and their size. Add the sour cream and Parmesan cheese, and mix well. Season with salt and pepper to taste; add the minced herbs and grated garlic. Serve hot with the tongue and olive stew.

NOTES

From the author:

You can use any kind of potatoes for this; I prefer red pototoes

45

I Must Not Be a Vampire!
Garlic, One of My Favorite Ingredients

I really do love garlic, but besides that, there is the funny association between this pungent vegetable and vampires. And because I was born and raised in Romania, I can not write about my life there without talking about everyone's favorite father of the vampires: Count Dracula! It is always a source of fun for me how people can create a whole cult around such an obviously fictional character. Or is he? Well, Count Dracula himself is not a fictional character. There was a man, the ruler of Valachia, a part of Romania located a little south of Transylvania, named Vlad Tepes, which literarily means Vlad the Impaler. His father was Vlad Dracul, meaning Vlad the devil, so the son, Vlad Tepes, was also known as Vlad Draculea, which means son of the devil. He is the real Count Dracula, born in Transylvania, where his castle still exists today. He was the inspiration behind the fictional Count Dracula brought alive in many books and movies, my favorite being Bram Stoker's *Dracula*. However, the real story behind the whole vampire craze belongs to a countess, who lived later in the late fifteen hundreds through early sixteen hundreds, named Elizabeth de Bathory. She was the one who killed a lot of young women in a very unusual way and disposed of the bodies in the forests, fields, and streams, causing locals to believe there was a strange creature lurking about at night killing unsuspecting people. The story that emerged about the undead Count Dracula and his evil ways was, more likely, a combination of these two real people and their real-life bad deeds. And, as we all know, one of the ways to repel a vampire is with garlic. Since I love garlic so much and use it in just about any dish I make my American friends have jokingly concluded that I am more than likely not a vampire, even though I was born in the country of their origins. But then again, I may be a vampire, but one that is immune to the effects of garlic. Now that is something to think about, especially right before bedtime… All joking aside, and all colorful vampire stories not withstanding, garlic really is one of my favorite ingredients. Its strong and distinct flavor can transform any savory dish from good to excellent. In Romania, besides the regular garlic, we had green garlic, which looks a lot like green onion and has a milder, sweeter flavor than the regular garlic. We used it a lot in fresh salads and other recipes that called for green onions as a way to boost flavor. Since I moved here, I haven't seen green garlic again, but I make good use of the regular garlic as often as I can. The other wonderful thing about garlic is that it has health benefits, and can be used for things such as lowering cholesterol and even as a natural antibiotic. So if you're not a big garlic fan, give it a second look. You might find this potent little vegetable a great ally in making better tasting foods! Here's a little recipe to get you warmed up to the idea.

Roasted Garlic Soup

30 garlic cloves, slightly smashed, skin on

12 garlic cloves, minced

3 shallots, halved and thinly sliced

1 14.5 oz can diced tomatoes

1 tsp dried basil

1 quart (4 cups) chicken broth, heated

½ cup cream

½ cup minced fresh parsley

2 tbsp lemon juice

Olive oil

Butter

Salt and pepper

Preheat oven to 375 degrees. Place 30 garlic cloves in a baking dish drizzle with 2 to 3 tablespoons of olive oil and some salt and mix to coat. Cover the baking dish with aluminum foil and place it in the preheated oven for 30 to 45 minutes until the garlic is golden brown and tender. Remove from the oven, and let the garlic cool. When cooled, squeeze the garlic between your fingertips to remove the roasted cloves. Place them into a bowl, and set it aside. In the meantime, melt 2 tablespoons of butter and 1 tablespoon olive oil in a large saucepan over medium heat. Add the shallots, and cook until translucent. Add

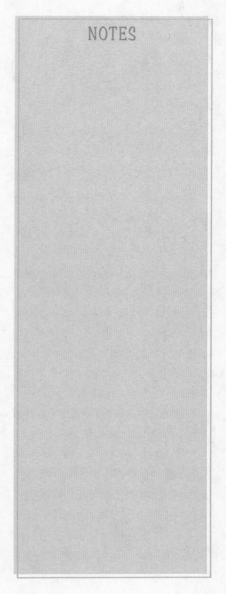

NOTES

49

NOTES

the minced garlic, and cook for another minute. Add the roasted garlic, and cook together for 2 more minutes. Add the diced tomatoes, dried basil, and the chicken broth, and simmer together for about 15 to 20 minutes. Working in 2 or 3 batches, puree the soup into a food processor until very smooth. Return the soup to the saucepan, bring to a gentle simmer, add the cream, and cook for 3 to 5 minutes. Remove from the heat, check for seasoning, mix in the fresh parsley and fresh lemon juice, and serve.

Beware of the Greeks

That expression usually refers to the famous Trojan horse that brought the never-conquered Troy to their knees. I refer to it a little jokingly to talk about the oh-so-yummy Greek influenced dishes that will add to your waistline but make you so very happy in the process. Even though Romania is part of the eastern side of Europe, we made plenty of Greek and Mediterranean influenced dishes, which always stood up to their delicious reputation. The two dishes I liked the most were variations of Moussaka and Spanakopita. The first dish actually has its origins in the Ottoman Empire, but the Greeks were the ones that made it very popular. Their version includes layers of eggplant, also known as aubergine, and meat, usually ground lamb, topped with a white sauce usually made of rue and milk, and then baked. The second dish is a Greek spinach pie, which consists of layers of phyllo dough topped with a mixture of spinach and cheese and then covered with more phyllo dough and baked. Sometimes the same filling is placed inside phyllo dough triangles, and I believe that was the influence for the Romanian version of spanakopita, except we made our triangles bigger and filled them either with cheese or meat, usually beef or pork. The Romanian version of moussaka most of the time had layers of potato slices instead of eggplant because potatoes were more readily available in the cold months which is when we usually made this dish. The meat filling was usually ground pork and very rarely beef or lamb, mixed with tomatoes, spices, and rice. If we made the dish in the summer, we did stay true to the Greek version and used eggplant, but we never topped our moussaka with the white sauce. Whatever the version, eggplant or potatoes, lamb or beef, spinach or cheese, those two dishes are always so delicious that you will come back for more. Here's my version of those Greek inspired yummies.

Moussaka

3 to 4 medium-sized eggplants

1 ½ lb ground lamb

1 large red onion, finely diced

2 medium leeks, white and light green parts only, finely chopped

4 to 6 large garlic cloves, minced

1 14.5 oz can diced tomatoes

3 Roma tomatoes, diced

4 Roma tomatoes, sliced

2 tbsp tomato paste

1 bunch kale, stems removed and finely chopped

1 cup chopped spinach

1 cup red wine, room temperature

¼ cup cream

1 cup minced fresh parsley

2 tbsp breadcrumbs

2 tsp dried oregano

2 tsp dried dill

1 bay leaf

½ tsp nutmeg

1 cup kefalotyri cheese, grated

Olive oil

Butter

Salt and pepper to taste

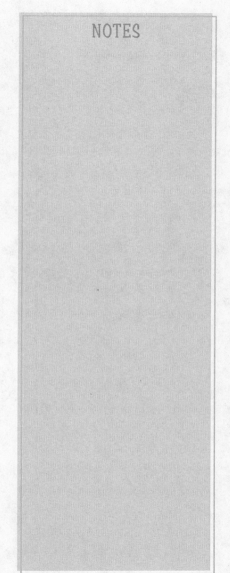

NOTES

Preheat oven to 400 degrees. Slice the eggplant long ways in slices about ½ inch thick. Place the eggplant on a large sheet pan, brush with olive oil, season with salt, and bake until softened, but not mushy, about 20 to 30 minutes. Remove from the oven, place the slices on the rack that comes with the sheet pan, place the rack back on the sheet pan, and allow the eggplant to drain. Reduce the oven to 350 degrees. Place a large sauté pan on medium to high heat, and add 2 tablespoons of olive oil and 1 tablespoon of butter. When hot but not smoking, add the onions and leeks, and sauté until soft for about 5 minutes. Season with salt, add the garlic, and cook for another minute. Add the ground lamb, and break it with a wooden spoon. Cook the lamb, onions, leeks, and garlic for about 5 minutes, mixing often. Add the wine, oregano, dill, bay leaf, nutmeg, salt and pepper to taste, mix and bring to a boil. Turn down the heat to medium-low, cover and simmer for about 30 minutes. After that time, add the canned tomatoes, roma tomatoes and tomato paste, and mix well to incorporate. Add the kale, cover and cook until the liquid is absorbed. Add the cream and spinach, mix and cook for another 5 minutes. Remove from heat, add the minced parsley, and check for seasoning. Set the mixture aside to cool. In the meantime, spray an ovenproof dish with cooking spray. Spread the breadcrumbs evenly on the bottom. Place 1 layer of the eggplant on top of the bread crumbs. Spread half of the lamb mixture on top of the eggplant evenly. Layer more eggplant slices on top, then add the rest of the lamb mixture. Top with the tomato slices, then sprinkle generously with the shredded cheese. Bake in the 350-degree oven for about 1 hour. Let it rest and cool slightly before serving. If it is slightly cooled, it will make the cutting easier.

NOTES

From the author:

If you're topping the moussaka with the white sauce, pour it over the top and sprinkle with cheese. Omit the tomato slices.

Personally, I don't top my moussaka with the white or béchamel sauce, but for those of you who want to, here's a recipe for it.

NOTES

From the author:

The measurements for this sauce vary, so I came up with my own base ratio that can be multiplied according to the amount of sauce you want to make: 1 tablespoon of butter to 1 tablespoon flour to 10 tablespoons of milk.

Béchamel (White) Sauce

1 stick of butter (8 tbsp) room temp
½ cup (8 tbsp) flour
5 cups whole milk, hot
1 cup grated Parmesan, Pecorino Romano,
    or whatever cheese you like
1 tsp nutmeg
Salt and pepper to taste

In a large saucepan, heat the butter on medium heat, being careful not to burn it. Add the flour, little by little, mixing constantly with a wire whisk. Season with salt and pepper; start adding the hot milk slowly, continuing to whisk. Add the nutmeg, and keep whisking. Cook the sauce on low to medium heat for about 5 to 7 minutes, mixing constantly. Remove from heat, and whisk in the cheese. Pour over the moussaka before baking, or use it to make a variety of other dishes.

Spanakopita Triangles

2 lb (4 cups) spinach

1 large red onion, finely diced

1 leek, white and light green parts only, finely chopped

1 bunch green onion, finely chopped

4 large garlic cloves, minced

1 cup minced fresh parsley

1 cup crumbled feta cheese

½ cup grated kefalotyri cheese

2 eggs

2 tbsp heavy cream

2 tsp dried oregano

16 sheets phyllo dough

Butter

Olive oil

Salt and pepper to taste

Preheat oven to 350 degrees. In a large sauté pan, heat 2 tablespoons of olive oil and 1 tablespoon of butter on medium heat until hot but not smoking. Add the onions, leeks, and green onions, and sauté until tender, about 5 minutes. Season with salt and pepper, add 1 teaspoon of dried oregano and the garlic, and cook for another minute. Add the spinach and parsley, and sauté until the spinach is wilted. Season again if necessary, remove from the

NOTES

NOTES

heat, and set aside to cool. Add the feta cheese, kefalotyri cheese, eggs, and cream to a bowl, and mix until very well incorporated. Season with salt and pepper, then add the spinach mixture and mix to incorporate. Set aside. Spray a large sheet pan with some cooking spray. Melt together about 6 tablespoons of butter and 1 teaspoon dried oregano. Layer 4 sheets of phyllo dough one on top of each other, lightly brushing each sheet with some of the melted butter mixture. Cut the sheets in half long ways. Repeat with the remaining phyllo sheets. You should have 8 phyllo strips, 4 layers deep each strip. Place about 2 tablespoons of spinach and cheese mixture in the far left corner of one of the long strips of buttered phyllo sheets. Start folding the corner over to form a triangle. Continue folding, overlapping in a triangle shape until you come to the end of the strip. Fold the last corner under, and place the triangle on the sheet pan. Repeat with all remaining phyllo strips. When finished, lightly brush the top of each triangle with some melted butter, place in the preheated oven, and bake until golden brown for about 30 to 40 minutes.

Phyllo Triangles
❤ With Meat ❤

1 lb ground beef or lamb

1 red onion, finely chopped

1 leek white and light green parts only, finely chopped

4 large garlic cloves, minced

1 cup chopped spinach

1 cup chopped fresh parsley

½ cup chopped fresh dill

1 cup red wine, room temp

1 tbsp-dried oregano

16 sheets phyllo dough

6 tbsp butter melted

Salt and pepper to taste

Olive oil

Butter

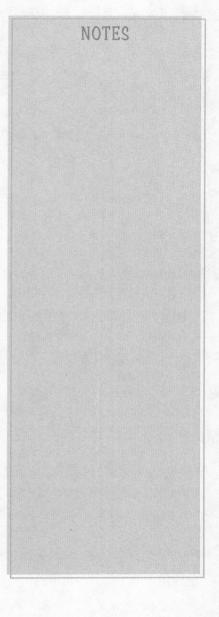

NOTES

Preheat oven to 350 degrees. In a large sauté pan, heat 2 tablespoons of olive oil and 1 tablespoon of butter on medium heat until hot but not smoking. Add the onions and leeks, and sauté until tender, about 5 minutes. Season with salt and pepper, add the garlic, and sauté for another minute. Add the meat, break up with a wooden spoon, season again, and cook for about 7 minutes, mixing from time to time. Add the wine and oregano, and simmer until

NOTES

the liquid is evaporated. Add the spinach and parsley, and cook for about 5 minutes. Check for seasoning, remove from heat, and set aside to cool. Assemble the triangles like in the spanakopita recipe, and bake in the preheated oven until golden brown, about 30 to 40 minutes.

❤ With Cheese ❤

1 cup (8 oz) cream cheese
1 cup (8 oz) ricotta cheese
1 cup (8 oz) grated Parmesan cheese
1 cup (8 oz) grated pecorino romano cheese
2 eggs
¼ cup breadcrumbs
1 tbsp country Dijon mustard
16 sheets phyllo dough
6 tbsp butter melted
2 tbsp minced fresh parsley
1 tbsp minced fresh dill
Salt and pepper to taste

Preheat oven to 350 degrees. Mix all the ingredients in a bowl until well incorporated. Season with salt and pepper and set aside. Assemble the phyllo triangles the same as in the meat recipe, and bake in the preheated oven for 30 to 40 minutes until golden brown.

Heard It through the Grapevine: Making Wine Really Is a Lot of Fun

When I lived in Romania, mid to late spring and early to mid fall were my favorite times of the year. Winters were hard and long, and heat in our homes was rationed and sometimes nonexistent. Winter many times lasted through March and sometimes even early April, which made late April and May a beautiful time of renewal. The sun shined and was warm again, the spring flowers were in bloom, and the air was clean, crisp, and clear. September and October were also a joy for me. Maybe because I knew November was coming with its cold weather and constant misty rain that seemed to chill all the way to the bone. So I guess I was appreciative of the balmy weather, the multicolored leaves on the trees, and the soft winds. The other fun thing in the fall was the making of the wine at my fraternal grandparents' home. They had a small vineyard, but it made a good amount of good wine, and I really enjoyed going over there and being involved in the process. First there was the gathering of the grapes, which was always fun because my cousin and I got to eat more than our share of the sweet bounty. Then there was the fun of watching my father and my uncle take turns cranking the handle on the small, manual wine press and holding the big metal buckets under the spigot while they were getting full of the sweet, red grape juice. I don't know much about what happened next, how the juice became the wine, but later in the days that followed, I could smell and hear the fermentation going on in the big, wooden barrels under the shed. The whole process was a lot of work, but it was always a lot of fun as well, and we always got to eat something good at the end of the day. The more popular contenders were fire-roasted, fresh corn on the cob, which we actually cooked on a makeshift grill that consisted of dry wood sticks placed directly on the ground and was surrounded by a few big rocks topped with some kind of metal mesh. Sometimes we also had a big fresh salad and a mushroom dish, which was basically our version of béchamel or white sauce with boiled mushrooms. It doesn't sound like much, but the corn was just picked, the mushrooms were wild and fresh, usually picked from a field somewhere in the village, and the salad was made with fresh vegetables from my grandmother's garden. I also think everything tasted so great because, by the time dinner time came, we were all so tired from all the work and extremely hungry! Here are two recipes inspired from those times.

Green Salad with Simple Vinaigrette

1 large head red leaf lettuce, coarsely chopped
2 large vine ripened tomatoes, cored, halved, and sliced
1 large seedless European cucumber, halved, and sliced
6 or 8 red radishes, sliced
½ red onion, thinly sliced
½ cup olive oil
¼ cup red wine vinegar
Salt and pepper

Whisk the olive oil, red wine vinegar, salt, and pepper in a large bowl until well incorporated. Mix the lettuce and vegetables together in a large salad bowl, and season with salt and pepper to taste. Serve dressed with some of the vinaigrette.

NOTES

Wild Mushrooms with White Sauce (Ciulama)

2 lb wild mushrooms, cleaned and cut in large chunks
1½ sticks butter-
8 tbsp flour
1 large onion, peeled and quartered
5 cups chicken broth, heated
1 bay leaf
1 cup minced fresh parsley
½ cup grated Parmesan cheese
Olive oil
Salt and pepper

Heat 4 tablespoons of butter and 2 tablespoons of olive oil in a large sauté pan until hot. Add the mushrooms, and cook until slightly browned. Add the chicken broth, bay leaf, and onion, and bring to a boil. Turn down the heat, and simmer for 15 to 20 minutes. In the meantime, add 1 stick of butter to a large saucepan with tall sides. When the butter is melted and starting to bubble, start adding the flour a little at the time, whisking constantly. Cook the flour, whisking for about 1 or 2 minutes. Take the bay leaf and onion out of the mushroom broth, and start slowly adding the mushroom broth along with the mushrooms into the butter and flour mixture. Continue adding and whisking until all the mushroom broth is added. The sauce should start to thicken right away. Continue simmering everything together, whisking constantly for an additional 3 to 5 minutes. Remove from the heat, add the cheese and the fresh parsley, and serve hot.

NOTES

Life Takes an Unexpected Turn: A Very Different Land Is Calling

In 1981, after over forty years of domination, the communist iron curtain finally started to fall all over Eastern Europe! In nation after nation, the people's restlessness and desire for freedom could no longer be contained. In December 1989, freedom came to Romania! It was a time of both joy and sorrow for all of us as, on one hand, we became free, but on the other, we saw hundreds of young men and women die at the hands of the army. For many days after the Revolution broke out, the army stayed loyal to Ceausescu, the Romanian communist leader, but after a while, they turned. They decided he, along with his family and close political sympathizers, were traitors and tyrants, responsible for cruelty and genocide against the Romanian people. He was caught and tried in a military-style courtroom. Found guilty, he was sentenced to death, and all of us watched his and his wife's execution on national TV. As communism fell, the borders were opened. An opportunity presented itself, and I crossed the ocean and landed in America in December 1992, exactly three years after the Revolution.

As you might imagine, we cooked and ate many other dishes in the time I lived in Romania, but the ones I have given you so far are some of my very favorite. I will be giving you more of them in the next chapters as I describe new and exciting adventures in my new home: America!

SECTION 2

Endless Possibilities: My Eclectic Style & Falling in Love with Food All over Again

Please Tell Me That Is Not a Grocery Store!

Before coming to America, I stayed in Paris for three months. I honestly believe that was a divine intervention because, had I gone straight to the US, I think the culture shock would've been too much to handle. Yes, France was very different—abundant and free—but it was still Europe! Slowly, I started to learn new things about what it was like to live a life of freedom, a life where you could actually buy anything you needed and not go without. Even if you didn't have a lot of money, things had different levels of expense, so there wasn't much I couldn't get. Things were wonderful; I was like a kid in a candy store, and the candy was everything from things to people to culture to the beauty of this most romantic town in the world. I saw the Eiffel tower for the first time on a warm, balmy September night. It looked as if it was made of gold, a great giant towering over the city, protective and strong. I had never imagined that life could be like that. And then there was the food… You have never really tasted French onion soup unless you ate it in Paris! And French bread… Oh, my! My weakness—bread—and there it was in every shape, every form, and every taste you can imagine! What, no three-hour lines for bread? Hmm… It was different, all right! This newfound abundance of flavors got me going, and I decided to start cooking again. And so I went to the grocery store. I will always remember walking into that store because I stopped dead in my tracks. There they were, row after row of shelves full of things I knew about but only dreamed of eating, things I'd never seen, and things I didn't even know existed. And then there was the fresh meat and seafood section with the kind of selections one can only dream of. But it didn't stop there. There was the deli section and pastry section, fresh produce, every kind of drink imaginable and unimaginable—for me at least. Wow, I'm getting dizzy just remembering what it was like. There is one thing I should mention though. There probably wouldn't have been such a big shock had I gone to a small food market. But I went to Auchan, which is an enormous retail store on the same level as Costco or Sam's Club. Still, it wasn't just the size; what got me the most was the selection, and that is true of any grocery store anywhere in the west. That will always be one of the most formidable experiences of my life!

Soon after, I came to America and landed in Texas, the state that was to become my permanent home, but Paris was a great interlude, a bridge, so to speak, that closed the gap between the world I came from and the one I would now live in. So as a tribute to that beautiful city, here's a recipe I love to make.

French Onion Soup

1 large red onion, cut in quarters, then sliced

1 large yellow onion, cut in quarters, then sliced

1 large white onion, cut in quarters, then sliced

1 large shallot, cut in half, then sliced

4 tbsp butter

4 cups vegetable broth, warm

4 cups beef broth, warm

1 cup white wine

¼ cup balsamic vinegar

4 thick slices French baguette, cut on the bias, and lightly toasted

8 oz (1 cup) Gruyere cheese, grated, and divided in 4 parts

1 bay leaf

1 tsp herbs de Provence

Olive oil

Salt and pepper

NOTES

Preheat oven to 400 degrees. Brush the bread slices very lightly with olive oil, and toast in the oven on the middle rack until light-golden brown. Remove promptly, and set the oven on broil. In a large Dutch oven, set on medium-high heat, melt the butter and 2 tablespoons of olive oil until hot but not smoking. Add the onions, shallots, and bay leaf;

NOTES

season with salt and pepper to taste, turn the heat down to med-low, and sauté the onions until they turn a golden brown and caramelize, about 30 to 45 minutes, mixing often. When the onions are cooked, add the balsamic vinegar to deglaze the pan. Simmer for about 5 minutes. Add the wine, and simmer for about 10 to 15 minutes. Add the vegetable and beef broth, herbs de Provence, salt and pepper to taste, and simmer uncovered for 20 minutes. Remove from the heat, take the bay leaf out, and ladle the soup in 4 large ramekins. Place one slice of bread on top of each ramekin, and sprinkle each with 2 ounces of cheese. Gently place the ramekins on the oven rack close to the top, and broil until the cheese is golden brown, about 5 minutes. Watch it carefully so the cheese does not burn. Serve hot.

Everything Is Bigger in Texas

It really is! Everything! From wide-open spaces to their Stetson cowboy hats to the food servings! The first town I lived in was Houston. The largest city in Texas and fourth largest in the nation, Houston has a wide variety of living to offer. Among its variety are the restaurants, which are many and varied, from little holes in the wall to large, five-star, expensive establishments! Almost as soon as I arrived, I got a job, a small apartment, an even smaller car, and I started experimenting with food! Here the sky was the limit. I had at my disposal all kinds of meat, produce, spices, fruits, anything and everything I would ever want. I started reading cookbooks, reading about American food, and watching cooking shows. Soon I noticed that the food I was making was not really a certain style, and that was because I liked experimenting and using whatever I liked at the moment, so the best way to describe what emerged was eclectic. My influence was my Romanian background, the Mediterranean style, and what I was learning from watching cooking shows and developing my techniques. Since I was single, I didn't make big, complicated dishes. My favorite things to make were soups and salads, so I came up with several recipes for both. Here are some of my favorites.

NOTES

From the author:

Kohlrabi is a very firm vegetable of the cabbage family and it is readily available in most grocery stores. It can also be consumed raw as a snack.

A food mill can be used here instead of the food processor to pure the vegetables.

SOUPS

Summer and Winter Cream Soup

❤ Summer ❤

1 head cauliflower, florets pulled apart

2 broccoli stocks, florets pulled apart

8 to 10 medium-sized white cap mushrooms, peeled and cut in half

1 turnip, peeled and cut in large cubes

1 large parsnip, peeled and cut in cubes

1 large white onion, cut in half and sliced thick

3 heads white kohlrabi, peeled and cubed

8 large garlic cloves, slightly smashed, but kept in the skin

1 cup fresh minced parsley

1 quart chicken broth, warm

1 tbsp butter

½ cup heavy cream, warm

1 tbsp lemon juice

Olive oil

Salt and pepper to taste

Preheat the oven to 400 degrees. Place the vegetables and the garlic on a sheet pan in a single layer, sprinkle with salt and some olive oil, mix to coat, and roast in the preheated oven for 20 to 30 minutes until golden brown. Do not overcrowd the pan. If needed, use 2 pans, and roast them at the same time. In the meantime, bring the chicken broth to a boil. When the vegetables are ready, take them out of the oven and let them cool a little. Take garlic out of the skin, and place it, along with the rest of the vegetables, in a large food processor. Puree until very smooth. Work in batches if necessary. Pour the puree in a medium-sized, tall saucepan, and place it on low heat. Start adding the hot chicken broth, one ladle at the time, until the desired consistency, mixing continually. When the desired consistency is reached, check for seasoning, and mix in the cream and butter. Simmer gently for 5 minutes, continuing to mix. Remove from heat, add the lemon juice and fresh parsley, mix, cover, and let it rest for a few minutes. Serve hot.

NOTES

❤ Winter ❤

2 medium-sized, red beats, peeled and cubed

2 large maroon carrots, peeled and cubed

2 portabella mushrooms, peeled and cubed

1 sweet potato, peeled and cubed

1 large yellow squash, peeled and cubed

3 heads red kohlrabi, peeled and cubed

1 red onion cut in half and sliced thick

8 large garlic cloves, slightly smashed, but kept in the skin

1/3 cup minced fresh cilantro

1 quart beef broth, heated

1 tbsp butter

½ cup heavy cream warm

1 tbsp lemon juice

Olive oil

Salt and pepper to taste

Prepare exactly the same as the previous recipe.

Butternut Squash Cream Soup

2 lbs butternut squash, cubed

2 medium-sized shallots, cut in half and sliced thick

2 cups chicken broth, heated

½ cup heavy cream, warm

½ tsp grated nutmeg

½ cup minced fresh parsley

Olive oil

Salt and pepper to taste

Preheat oven to 400 degrees. Place the cubed squash and the thick slices of shallots on a large sheet pan. Sprinkle with olive oil, about 2 tablespoons, and salt to taste, mix to coat, and bake for about 20 minutes until golden brown and soft. Transfer the cooked butternut squash and shallots to a food processor, and puree until very smooth. Transfer to a saucepan on low heat and warm up, stirring often. Season with salt and pepper, add the chicken broth, one ladle at the time, and continue mixing. Add the nutmeg and more salt and pepper if necessary, and stir. Add the warm cream and simmer gently for about 5 minutes. Turn off the heat, and add the fresh parsley. Stir and serve warm.

NOTES

From the author:

You can find the squash already cubed in the store.

NOTES

Turkey Meatball Soup

1 lb ground turkey

1 egg, lightly beaten

1 or 2 quarts chicken broth heated

1 yellow onion, diced

4 garlic cloves, mined

1 small red bell pepper, quartered and sliced

1 small yellow bell pepper, quartered and sliced

½ red cabbage, quartered and thinly sliced

6 potatoes, peeled and cut in small cubes

1 cup chopped kale

1 cup chopped fresh parsley

3 tbsp cream, warm

2 tbsp fresh lemon juice

Olive oil

Butter

Salt and pepper

In a bowl, mix the ground turkey with the beaten egg, some salt and pepper, and ½ cup of fresh parsley. Start making turkey meatballs about ½ inch in diameter, and set them on a plate. In a Dutch oven, heat 2 tablespoons of butter and 1 tablespoon of olive oil until hot. Add the onion, and sauté for about 2 minutes. Add the bell peppers and garlic, season with salt and pepper, and sauté for about

3 minutes. Add the potatoes and 1 quart heated chicken broth. Season with salt and pepper, and bring to a boil. Reduce the heat, add the cabbage, and let it simmer for a couple of minutes. Start adding the meatballs one at a time until they are all added. Simmer for 5 to 7 minutes. Add the chopped kale, chopped parsley, and cream, and more broth if necessary. Mix gently, simmer for 1 minute, and remove from the heat. Add 1 tablespoon of butter and the lemon juice; check for seasoning, mix, and serve.

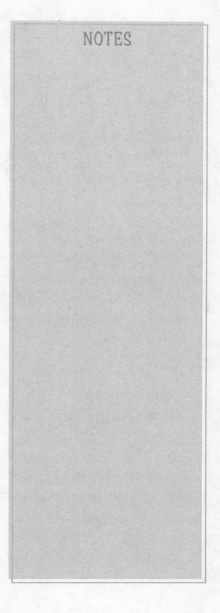

NOTES

NOTES

Italian Sausage Soup with Kale and Spinach

4 mild Italian sausages, skin removed, and broken into
   small bite size pieces
1 red onion, finely chopped
2 small leeks, white part only, finely chopped
2 large carrots, finely chopped
6 med to large mushrooms, finely chopped
6 fresh garlic cloves, minced
White wine
2 cups chopped spinach
2 cups chopped kale
6 med red potatoes, sliced in small pieces
2 quarts chicken stock
1 cup heavy cream, warm
4 tbsp butter
Olive oil
1 cup minced fresh parsley
½ cup minced fresh dill

In a medium to large sized pot, heat 2 tablespoons of olive oil until hot but not smoking. Add the sausage, and cook for about 5 minutes on medium-high heat. Remove the sausage and to the same pot add 1 tbsp each olive oil and butter. Add the onion, leeks, carrots and mushrooms, and cook until translucent. Add the garlic, and cook another minute. Add enough wine to cover the vegetables, and cook until the wine evaporates. Take the pot off the heat, and let the veggies cool down a little. Add the cooked veggies to a food processor, and process until very smooth. Place the pot over medium-high heat, add the paste, and then add all the chicken stock slowly and bring to a low boil. Add the potatoes and kale, and boil for 2 to 3 minutes. Add the sausage and the spinach, and simmer gently together for 5 more minutes. Remove from heat, and add the cream and the fresh herbs. Serve hot.

NOTES

NOTES

SALADS

Simple Chunky Summer Salad with Lemon-Balsamic Vinegar Vinaigrette

2 English cucumbers
2 large vine ripped tomatoes
2 medium avocados, ripe but still hard to the touch
2 tbsp lemon juice
2 tbsp balsamic vinegar
¼ cup olive oil
½ cup chopped fresh parsley
Salt and pepper to taste

Peel the cucumber and avocados; then cut the first 3 ingredients into medium-sized chunks. Place in a salad bowl and mix together well. Add salt and pepper to taste. In a small bowl, whisk together the lemon juice, balsamic vinegar, and olive oil. Season with salt and pepper. Pour over the veggies, add the chopped parsley and mix. Serve chilled.

Spinach Salad, No Dressing Required

2 packed cups fresh baby spinach

½ red onion cut in half then very thinly sliced

1 red bell pepper, quartered and sliced

1 seedless English cucumber, halved and sliced

½ cup cherry or grape tomatoes, halved

½ cup pitted kalamatta olives, halved

2 roasted red bell peppers in water, drained and thinly sliced

1 large avocado, quartered and sliced

½ cup crumbled Feta cheese

Mix all ingredients 1 through 8 together in a large salad bowl. Season with salt and pepper to taste. Serve with Feta cheese sprinkled on top. Because of the combination of roasted bell peppers, kalamatta olives, and Feta cheese, this salad does not need any dressing.

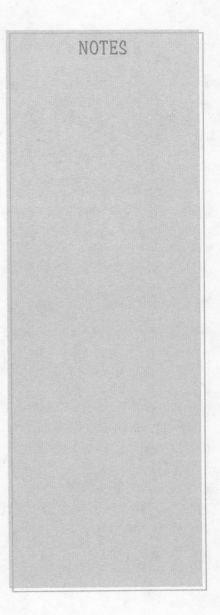

NOTES

NOTES

Easy Chicken Salad

1 ½ cups cubed or shredded cooked rotisserie chicken
1 head romaine hearts lettuce, sliced thin
1/2 cup watercress, sliced thin
½ cup large green olives, halved
1 seedless English cucumber, halved and sliced
½ cup cherry tomatoes, halved
½ cup chopped chives
1 avocado, halved and sliced

In a salad bowl, mix together ingredients 2 through 7. Add the chicken and avocado and toss gently to incorporate. Serve with creamy goat cheese vinaigrette.

Creamy Goat Cheese Vinaigrette

1 small to medium lemon, juiced
1 tbsp champagne or white wine vinegar
¼ cup olive oil
1 oz crumbled goat cheese
Salt and pepper to taste

In a small food processor, mix the goat cheese and olive oil together until smooth. With the processor on, add the lemon juice and vinegar slowly until all is incorporated. Season to taste with salt and pepper, and serve with the chicken salad.

NOTES

Four Bean Salad with Lemon-Lime Vinaigrette

1 can white kidney (cannellini) beans
1 can garbanzo beans
1 can red kidney beans
1 package shelled soybeans
1 bunch green onions, finely chopped
1 cup very finely chopped fresh dill and parsley
Salt to taste

Dressing:
The juice from 1 large lemon and 2 limes
The zest from 1 lemon and 1 lime
1 tbsp minced parsley
1 tbsp minced dill
½ cup + 1 tbsp olive oil
1 tsp mayo
Salt and pepper to taste

Rinse all the beans with cold water and drain. In a large salad bowl, combine all the beans with the green onions and fresh dill and parsley. Season with salt and pepper, mix well, and set aside. In a small bowl that has a tight lid, add the lemon and lime juice and zest, olive oil, the fresh herbs, mayo, and salt and pepper to taste. Cover tightly with the lid; then shake well to combine all the ingredients. Serve the bean salad cold, dressed with the vinaigrette. For a little kick, add ¼ tsp cayenne pepper to the dressing.

NOTES

Warm Lamb and Orzo Salad

4 lamb loin chops
8-10 large shrimp, peeled, devained
1 cup orzo pasta
½ cup white wine
½ cup kalamatta olives, halved
½ cup minced fresh parsley
1 heaping teaspoon of good mayo
The juice of half of lemon
¼ tsp cayenne pepper
1 tsp dried basil
Butter
Olive oil
1 tsp flour
Salt

Cook the orzo according to the package instructions. Set aside, covered to keep warm. In a sauté pan, heat 1 tablespoon of olive oil and 1 tablespoon of butter on medium-high heat until hot but not smoking. Add the lamb chops and cook on medium-high for 3 minutes per side. Add the wine, mix well, cover, and cook the lamb for about 5 more minutes. Meanwhile, add the cooked orzo to a salad bowl, add ½ tablespoon of butter, and mix well. Add the olives, parsley, mayo, and lemon juice, and mix well.

Remove the lamb, and cut in small pieces. To the sauce in the pan, add the flour, cayenne pepper, and dried basil, and cook together for about 2 minutes until sauce thickens. Add the lamb pieces to the orzo along with the pan sauce. In the same saucepan, add another tablespoon of butter and sauté the shrimp, covered for only 2 minutes. Remove promptly, chop, and add to the salad with the pan juices. Mix the salad together well and serve.

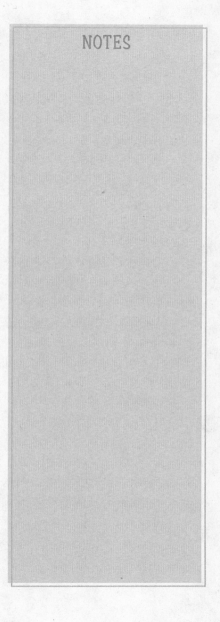

NOTES

Another Unexpected Turn: Cooking for Two

In July of 1995, two and a half years after I came to America, I became a Christian. A little over a year later, while I was at church one Sunday morning, I noticed a very striking and handsome man a few rows behind me. I liked him the moment I saw him, but at the time, I was very focused on my newfound spiritual life, and I really did not want anything to interfere with it. Although I was twenty-eight years old and really wanted to settle down and have a family, what I wanted more was to meet someone through divine intervention rather than on my own. I had already been through a failed marriage, and I did not want that to happen again. So I prayed! I asked God that if He wanted me to get married to bring someone in my life. That said, I stopped thinking about the handsome, well-dressed man I saw and tried to refocus my thoughts somewhere else. What I didn't know at the time was that the prayer I prayed had already been answered. The man I mentioned had noticed me too, and, as fate would have it, he prayed the same prayer with one small exception. He asked God to make a way for him to meet me, specifically, if that was the divine plan. I would say it was because only a couple of weeks later someone introduced us on a Sunday before the church service. Exactly seven weeks later, on December 7, 1996, we married. Some said—and I'm sure might still say it to this day—that we married too soon.

That can be true, but it wasn't for us. Today, thirteen years and two children later, we're still married, and although we've had our ups and downs, we always remember who put us together. That faith in the One who did is what keeps us strong even when we're not! Being married, I now had a reason to become better at what I loved to do: cooking! So I started watching even more cooking shows, reading even more cookbooks, and trying even harder to improve my cooking repertoire. My husband would tell you that he was impressed. He actually said to me once that he didn't expect to come home to a home-cooked meal each night, let alone a different dish every time. But I loved experimenting, and I loved his reaction to my food! One of the things I did was introduce him to new flavors and ingredients, things he had not eaten before. For example, as unusual as this might sound, before he met me, he'd never eaten lamb. I tried to cook just about everything, from beef and lamb to turkey, fish, and seafood! Here are some of the dishes I made for him in the beginning and all throughout our marriage.

Rack of Lamb with Basil, Garlic, and Sun-Dried Tomato Pesto

1 rack of lamb, trimmed and frenched

3 garlic cloves

½ cup fresh basil

6 sun-dried tomatoes in oil

¼ cup sun-dried tomato olive oil

Salt and pepper to taste

2 tbsp olive oil

1 tbsp butter

Preheat oven to 400 degrees. In a small food processor, add the garlic, basil, sun-dried tomatoes, and salt and pepper to taste. Start pulsing until everything becomes coarse. With the processor on, start drizzling in the sun-dried tomato olive oil until it is all incorporated. Reserve some pesto for serving. Place a large sauté pan on medium-high heat, and add 2 tablespoons of olive oil and 1 tablespoon of butter. Heat until hot but not smoking. In the meantime, season the lamb generously with salt and pepper on both sides. Add the lamb to the sauté pan, and sear on each side for 2 to 3 minutes. Place in the preheated oven and roast for 5 minutes. Remove from the oven, and let it cool just a few minutes. When slightly cooled, start spreading the pesto on the fat side of the rack. Place in

NOTES

From the author:

"Frenching" refers to scraping the meat off the tips of the bones. To trim, just cut off some of the fat from the top of the meat. Leave a little for flavor.

NOTES

the oven and roast for about 15 minutes for medium rare, which is about 145 degrees internal temperature. Let the lamb rest, covered for about 10 minutes before serving. When the lamb has rested, cut the rack in between each bone and serve with some of the reserved pesto.

Mediterranean Style Lamb Meatloaf

2 lbs ground lamb

1 large red onion, finely diced

1 large shallot, finely diced

4 large garlic cloves, minced

½ cup white wine

2 tsp dried oregano

6 white cap mushrooms, stems removed, peeled and
    diced

2 large garlic cloves, grated

1 cup finely chopped spinach

1 14.5 oz can diced tomatoes

2 tbsp tomato paste, thinned with 2 tbsp cream

1/3 cup red wine

½ cup crumbled feta cheese

2 eggs

½ cup breadcrumbs

1 bunch fresh parsley, minced

4 tbsp tomato paste

1 tbsp red wine

2 tbsp heavy cream

1 tbsp minced fresh parsley

Olive oil

Butter

Salt and pepper to taste

NOTES

NOTES

In a sauté pan on medium to high heat, melt 2 tablespoons of butter and 1 tablespoon of olive oil until hot but not smoking. Add the onions and shallots, and cook for about 3 to 5 minutes. Season with salt and pepper, add the mushrooms and the minced garlic, and cook for an additional 5 minutes. Add the white wine and dried oregano, and cook until the wine is evaporated. Season again if necessary, remove from heat, and let it cool. In the meantime, in a large bowl combine the ground lamb, grated garlic, spinach, diced tomatoes, and tomato paste, and mix together gently with a fork until well incorporated. Do not overwork the meat. In a small bowl, beat the eggs and the red wine, and add it to the meat. Add the breadcrumbs, the mushroom and onion mixture, and the parsley, and mix to incorporate. Add the feta cheese, salt and pepper to taste, and mix again until incorporated. Remember to do all the mixing gently with a fork. In a small bowl, mix together 4 tablespoons of tomato paste, 1 tablespoon of red wine, 2 tablespoons of heavy cream, and 1 tablespoon of minced, fresh parsley. Season with salt and pepper, and set aside. Divide the meat mixture in 2 equal parts on a large sheet pan lined with parchment paper or aluminum foil. Form each part into a loaf with your hands. Brush the top of each loaf with the tomato paste and cream mixture, place in the preheated oven, and bake for 40 to 45 minutes or until an instant thermometer inserted in the middle of each loaf reads 155 to 160 degrees. Let the loaves rest, covered, for a few minutes before serving.

Beef and Vegetables Meatloaf

2 lbs lean ground beef

1 red onion, chopped

6 garlic cloves, minced

2 large carrots, chopped

6 stocks celery, chopped

10 white cap mushrooms, sliced

1 cup chopped Swiss chard

1 cup chopped fresh parsley

1/2 cup chopped cilantro

1 can diced tomatoes

1/3 cup white wine

1 tbsp dried oregano

1 tbsp dried dill

Olive oil

Butter

Salt and pepper to taste

Preheat oven to 375 degrees. In a large sauté pan, heat 2 tablespoons of olive oil and 1 tablespoon of butter until hot but not smoking; then add the red onion and cook until softened. Add diced carrots, celery, and mushrooms, and cook until softened. Add minced fresh garlic, and cook for another 1 to 2 minutes then set aside. In a large bowl, add the beef, chard, fresh chopped parsley and

NOTES

99

NOTES

cilantro, diced tomatoes, wine, 2 tablespoons of olive oil, and the spices; then season with salt and pepper. Mix all ingredients together gently with a fork until well incorporated. Add the vegetable mixture, and mix again. Divide the meat in 2 equal parts on a sheet pan, form into loaves, and bake in the preheated oven 40 to 45 minutes until the inside temp reaches 155 to 160 degrees.

Ground Beef and Chicken Meatballs

1 lb ground beef

2 boneless, skinless chicken breasts cut in very small cubes

1 red onion, finely diced

6 garlic cloves, minced

¼ cup white wine

2 eggs

¼ cup Italian seasoned Panko bread crumbs

¼ cup milk

4 tbsp olive oil, or more

2 tbsp dried basil

2 tbsp dried parsley

Salt and cayenne pepper to taste

1 cup chopped fresh parsley

Preheat the oven to 350. In a medium saucepan, heat up 2 tablespoons of olive oil and 1 tablespoon of butter until hot but not smoking. Add the diced onion, and cook until translucent on medium high, about 2 to 3 minutes. Add the minced garlic, and season with dried basil, dried parsley, ½ teaspoon of cayenne pepper and salt to taste. Cook together for another minute. Add the wine, and cook until the liquid is reduced by half. Remove from heat and set aside to cool. In a large bowl, add the

NOTES

NOTES

ground beef, cubed chicken, eggs, breadcrumbs, milk, 2 tablespoons of olive oil, dried basil and parsley, cayenne pepper and fresh parsley. Mix together gently with a fork until well incorporated. Season with salt, add the cooked onion mixture, and mix again until well incorporated. If the mixture is too soft, add more bread crumbs so that meatballs can be formed. Form meatballs, about 1 ½ inches in diameter and set on a plate. In a large sauté pan, heat up 2 tablespoons of olive oil and one tablespoon of butter on medium high. When hot, add the meatballs one by one, and cook 2 minutes on each side. Cook in batches if necessary so the pan is not crowded and the meatballs can brown. Remove from the sauté pan, and arrange them on a sheet pan. Cook in the preheated oven for 15 to 20 minutes. Enjoy with your choice of sauce.

Pasta and Cabbage Sautéed in Butter with Bacon and Ground Beef

1 large green cabbage, steamed

1 large red onion, diced

1 large leek, white and light green parts only, diced

6 large garlic cloves, minced

½ cup white wine, room temp

1 lb ground beef

6 slices bacon, chopped

1 8 oz package egg noodles, cooked according to the directions on the package

½ cup grated Parmesan cheese

1 cup chopped fresh parsley

Olive oil

Butter

Salt and pepper to taste

Cut the cabbage in half, and remove the hard core. Bring some water to a boil in a large, tall pot fitted with a steam basket. When the water is boiling, place the cabbage in the steam basket over the boiling water, cover, and let it steam for 15 to 20 minutes depending upon the size of the cabbage. Remove promptly, and place it in ice water to stop the cooking process. Remove from the cold water, and allow the cabbage to drain for a few minutes. Cut

NOTES

From the author:

This is a dish I learned here in the states, but I believe it was originally a Polish dish called haluski. It usually consists of cabbage and pasta sautéed together in butter, but I came up with a more gourmet version by adding bacon and ground beef. Ground pork or turkey can be substituted.

103

NOTES

each half in half again; then slice it in ½ inch slices, and set it aside. Place a large sauté pan over medium-high heat, and add the bacon. Cook it until crisp, remove it, and set it aside. Remove all but 1 tablespoon of bacon grease from the sauté pan, and then add the ground beef and cook until browned, about 7 minutes. Remove and set aside. To the same pan, add 1 tablespoon of bacon grease, 2 tablespoons of butter, and 2 tablespoons of olive oil. Add the onions and the leeks, and cook for about 5 minutes, mixing often. Add the garlic, and cook for another minute. Add the sliced cabbage, another tablespoon of butter, salt and pepper to taste, mix, and cook for about 5 minutes. Add the wine, and cook until it is almost evaporated. Add the cooked ground beef, mix, and cook together for about 5 minutes. Add the noodles and the bacon, and cook for an additional 5 minutes. Check for seasoning, remove from the heat, and mix in the parsley and the cheese. Serve hot.

Stuffed Bell Peppers

1 lb ground beef

1 lb ground pork

4 red bell peppers, halved, seeds and ribs removed

1 red bell pepper, chopped

1 red onion, diced

1 leek, white and light green parts only, halved and thinly sliced

4 garlic cloves, minced

1 cup white wine, room temperature

2 eggs, lightly beaten

1 14.5 oz can diced tomatoes

1 14.5 oz can tomato sauce

2 tbsp tomato paste

2 tbsp cream

¾ cup panko breadcrumbs

1 cup chopped spinach

1 cup minced fresh parsley

2 tsp dried oregano

2 tsp dried basil

½ tsp cayenne pepper

½ cup crumbled goat cheese

Olive oil

Butter

Salt and pepper

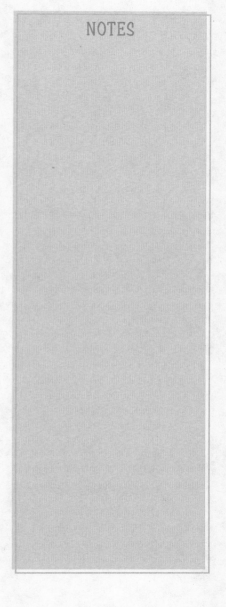

NOTES

NOTES

Preheat oven to 350 degrees. Heat 2 tablespoons of olive oil and 1 tablespoon of butter in a large sauté pan over medium heat until hot. Add the onions, leeks, and chopped red bell pepper, and cook until translucent, about 3 to 5 minutes. Season with salt and pepper, add the minced garlic, and cook for another minute. Add the wine, and cook until the liquid has reduced by half. Remove from the heat, and set aside to cool. To a large bowl, add the ground beef, ground pork, beaten eggs, diced tomatoes, and breadcrumbs. In a small bowl, mix the tomato paste and cream until smooth then add the mixture to the big bowl. Mix all the ingredients together gently with a fork until well incorporated. Add the onion, bell pepper and wine mixture, add salt and pepper to taste, dried herbs, cayenne pepper, and fresh parsley, and mix to incorporate. Fill the red pepper halves with an equal amount of the meat mixture, and arrange them in a shallow baking dish. Pour the tomato sauce all over the pepper halves, and sprinkle with some crumbled goat cheese. Cover loosely with aluminum foil, and bake for 30 minutes in the preheated 350-degree oven. Remove the foil and bake uncovered another 20 to 25 minutes until an instant thermometer inserted in the thickest part of the meat registers 155-160 degrees. Serve with sour cream.

Greek-Inspired Steak Dinner for Two

2 NY strip steaks, room temperature, seasoned with salt and light drizzle of olive oil

1 leek, white and light green parts only, finely chopped

1 med. shallot, finely chopped

1 med. to large red onion, finely chopped

6 garlic cloves, minced

1 med. to large eggplant cut in small cubes

10 to 12 crimini (mini portabella) mushrooms cut in small cubes

1 14.5 oz can diced tomatoes

½ cup white wine

1 tbsp-dried basil

1 tbsp-dried dill

¼ tsp cayenne pepper

1 tbsp butter cut in small pieces

Salt to taste

2 tbsp plain Greek style yogurt

1 tbsp lemon juice

1 long, English-style cucumber; peeled, seeded, grated and squeezed

2 fresh garlic cloves, finely grated

Salt to taste

1½ cups chicken broth, seasoned with 1 tsp each dried dill, basil, and garlic

NOTES

NOTES

1 cup couscous
½ cup grated Parmesan cheese
1 tbsp butter
Juice of ¼ lemon
1 cup minced fresh parsley
½ cup minced fresh basil

In a large sauté pan set on medium-high heat, add 3 tablespoons of olive oil, and then add the leeks, shallots, and onion. Sauté until translucent. Add 1 tablespoon of butter; then add the eggplant, mushrooms, and garlic. Cook together, mixing often until the eggplant is soft but not mushy. Add the diced tomatoes, and cook together for another few minutes. Add the wine and the dried spices, and cook until the wine is completely evaporated. Add the chopped butter, mix, cover, and set aside. Right before serving mix in some fresh herbs.

In a small saucepan, bring the seasoned chicken broth to a rolling boil. Add the couscous, remove from the heat, cover, and let it sit at least 5 minutes. Uncover, fluff with a fork, then add the Parmesan cheese, butter, lemon juice, and some of the fresh herbs; mix with the fork, and set aside.

In a small bowl, mix together the yogurt, lemon juice, cucumber, and garlic. Season with salt and pepper, add some fresh herbs, mix well, and set aside.

Heat a stovetop griddle or grill to high, reduce heat to med-high and cook the steaks 4 minutes per side. Remove, let them sit for about 5 minutes, then slice.

To serve, place some couscous on the bottom of the plate, add some eggplant mixture, top with the sliced steaks, and pour some of the yogurt sauce on top.

NOTES

NOTES

Pan-Seared Veal Chops with White Wine Sauce

2 medium to large veal chops, bone in
Olive oil
Butter
Salt
Pepper

Sauce:
Olive oil
½ white onion, finely chopped
4 shallots, finely chopped
6-8 large shitake mushrooms, sliced
12 small crimini (baby portabella) mushrooms, sliced
1 ½ cups white wine
½ cup cream, warm
¾ stick (6 tbsp) butter
½ cup each finely chopped parsley and cilantro
¼ cup finely chopped fresh basil

Season the veal chops on both sides with salt and pepper. In a large pan set over medium-high heat, heat about 2 tablespoons of olive oil until hot but not smoking. Add the veal chops, and sear on each side until golden brown, about 1 to 2 minutes per side. Remove and set aside. In the same pan, add ½ stick of butter and let it melt; then add the onion and the shallots, and cook until translucent. Add the mushrooms and cook until golden brown; then add the wine, and let it cook down about halfway. Reduce the heat to low, add the veal, cover, and let it cook together for about 15 to 20 minutes or until the veal internal temperature reaches 145 degrees for medium rare. If the sauce is reducing too fast, add a small amount of chicken broth and continue cooking. When the veal is cooked through, remove from the pan and set it aside; then add the warm cream, and let it cook down until the sauce has a thick consistency. Remove from heat, and add the chopped herbs and the rest of the butter to finish the sauce. Serve on top of the veal chops.

NOTES

NOTES

Oven-Baked Pork Chops

2 med. size pork chops, bone in
1 egg
1 tsp country Dijon mustard
2 tsp dried dill
1 tsp sea salt
1 and ½ cups seasoned panko Japanese bread crumbs
3 tbsp freshly grated peccorino Romano cheese

Preheat oven to 425. In a small bowl, beat together the egg, mustard, sea salt, and dried dill. Pour in a flat plate. On another plate combine the breadcrumbs and cheese. Set an ovenproof medium-sized sauté pan on the burner on high, and heat 2 tablespoons of olive oil until hot but not smoking. Season the pork chops with salt and pepper; then dredge each chop first through the egg and then through the breadcrumb mixture, on each side. Reduce heat to medium high, and cook the chops in the oil for about 2 minutes on each side until golden brown. Transfer the pan to the preheated oven and bake for 15 minutes. Let the chops rest a few minutes before serving.

Marinated Oven-Roasted Pork Loin with Creamy Mushroom Sauce

1 1.5 to 2 lb pork loin, marinated for at least 20 minutes
5 large white cap and 5 large mini portabella mushrooms sliced
½ cup white wine
3 tbsp heavy cream
Lemon juice
Fresh parsley and dill, finely chopped
1 large shallot, thinly sliced
4 large garlic cloves, minced

For the marinade:
   3 tbsp white wine
   ¼ cup olive oil
   4 garlic cloves
   6 leaves fresh basil
   ¼ cup fresh parsley
   Salt and freshly ground pepper to taste

Preheat the oven to 375. Place the pork loin in a shallow dish. In a small food processor, grind together all the marinade ingredients. Pour the marinade over the loin,

NOTES

NOTES

From the author:

This dish can be served with rice, salad, or anything you might like, but I prefer herbed potatoes. Recipe on next page.

making sure it is well covered, and let it marinate for at least 20 minutes, turning from time to time. When the 20 or more minutes have passed, place a large sauté pan on high heat, add 2 tablespoons of olive oil and 1 tablespoon of butter, and let it get very hot. Turn the heat down to medium-high, and add the pork loin. Cook on each side for about 2 to 3 minutes until golden brown. Remove the loin, and place it on a small sheet pan. Pour the remaining marinade on top, and roast in the preheated oven for about 30 to 35 minutes until the internal temperature reaches 150 degrees. Remove, and let it rest before slicing. In the meantime, place the same sauté pan back on medium heat, add 1 tablespoon of butter and 2 tablespoons of olive oil; then add the shallots and cook for about a minute, mixing often. Add the garlic and cook for another minute. Add the wine, making sure to scrape all the bits off the bottom of the pan. Cook until the wine reduces almost completely. Add the sliced mushrooms, and season with salt and pepper. Cook the mushrooms until the juices cook away. Add the cream, and cook for about a minute. Take away from the heat; add fresh parsley and dill, ½ tablespoon of butter, and 1 tablespoon of lemon juice. Mix well, and let it sit for a few minutes. Serve over the sliced loin.

Herbed Potatoes

8 medium-sized Yukon gold potatoes, peeled and
quartered
1 tbsp butter
2 tbsp butter, melted
2 tbsp olive oil
2 tbsp minced fresh dill
2 tbsp minced fresh parsley
2 tbsp lemon juice
1 tbsp lemon zest

Place the quartered potatoes in a large pot, cover with
cold water, and boil on high heat until tender but not too
soft. Drain, place them back in the pot, add 1 tablespoon
of butter, and cook together for 2 to 3 minutes. Whisk
together the melted butter, 2 tablespoons of olive oil, 2
tablespoons of lemon juice, 1 tablespoon of lemon zest,
and 2 tablespoons each of fresh dill and parsley, and pour
over the potatoes. Season with salt and pepper to taste,
gently mix, and serve with the pork loin.

NOTES

Laura Laird

NOTES

Oven-Roasted Pork and Cabbage with Sour Cream Sauce
❤ Simple Sour Cream Sauce ❤

1 8 oz tub light sour cream or crème fresh
¼ cup cream
4 oz light whipped cream cheese
3 tbsp chopped chives
Salt and pepper to taste

Mix together the first three ingredients in a small food processor until creamy. Add finely chopped chives, and season with salt and pepper to taste.

4 pork loin chops, 1 ½ to 2 inches thick, boneless
1 large white onion, diced
1 medium-sized green cabbage, finely chopped
1 cup tomato sauce
2 cups fat free Italian dressing
6 fresh garlic cloves, minced
1 cup chopped fresh parsley
Olive oil
Butter
Salt and pepper to taste

Marinate the pork chops in the Italian dressing for at least 30 minutes. Preheat the oven to 375 degrees. Heat 2 tablespoons of olive oil and 2 tablespoons of butter in a sauté pan until hot but not smoking. Add the meat, and sear for 2 minutes on each side until golden brown. Remove from the pan, and set it aside. In the same olive oil, add the finely diced onion and the chopped cabbage, and cook together until the cabbage is browned, not wilted. To achieve this, the oil needs to be pretty hot, but be careful not to burn the oil or the cabbage. Stir in the minced garlic, and season with salt and pepper. Set aside. Spray an ovenproof pan with cooking spray; then transfer the cabbage mixture to the bottom of the pan and spread evenly. Add the pork on top, add the tomato sauce, and roast in the preheated oven for about 20 to 25 minutes or until the inside temperature of the pork chops reaches 155 degrees. Take out of the oven; sprinkle with fresh, chopped parsley and serve with the sour cream sauce.

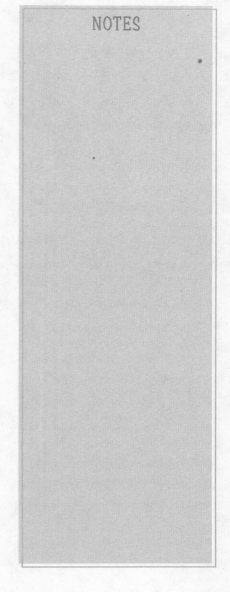

NOTES

Coq Au Vin

6 bacon slices, chopped

6 chicken thighs, skin on, bone in

1 red onion, sliced

2 large shallots, sliced

6 fresh garlic cloves, minced

1 head Napa cabbage, coarsely chopped

1 ½ cup white wine, room temperature

1 cup chicken broth, room temperature

Olive oil

Butter

½ cup minced fresh parsley

½ cup minced fresh dill

1 tbsp flour

1 tbsp butter, room temperature

3 tbsp butter

Salt and pepper to taste

Season the chicken thighs generously on each side with salt and pepper. In a large sauté pan set on medium-high heat, add the bacon and cook until crisp. Remove the bacon, and set it aside. Pour out all but 1 tablespoon of the bacon grease out of the pan, add 1 tablespoon of olive oil, and then add the chicken thighs to the pan. Brown the chicken on both sides on medium-high heat for about 5 minutes per side. Remove, and set aside. In the same pan, add another tablespoon of olive oil, add the onion and shallots, and cook together for about 3 to 5 minutes. Add the garlic, and cook for another minute. Add the cabbage; season, and cook for 5 minutes. Add the bacon and the chicken back to the pan then add the white wine and chicken stock. Turn the heat down to low, cover, and simmer for 30 to 45 minutes until the inside temperature of the chicken thighs reaches 160 degrees. When the chicken is done, remove it from the pan and add 2 tablespoons of butter and the fresh herbs to the sauce. Mix the soft butter and flour in a small bowl, and add the mixture to the sauce. Mix until the sauce starts to thicken, add the chicken back to the pan, and cook another 5 minutes on medium-high. Serve with herb-butter burgundy carrots and red potatoes.

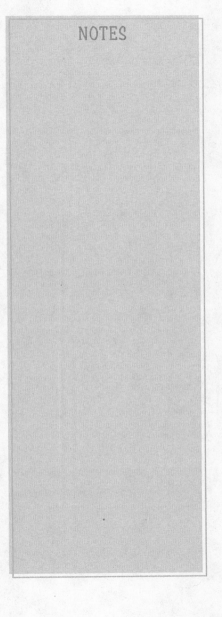

NOTES

Herb-Butter Maroon Carrots and Red Potatoes

6 small red potatoes cut in half
2 large burgundy carrots, peeled and cut on the bias in large chunks
4 tbsp butter
½ cup finely chopped fresh parsley and dill
2 tbsp heavy cream, warm
Salt and pepper to taste

Add the carrots and potatoes to a small saucepan, cover with cold water, bring to a boil, and cook for about 7 minutes or until the carrots and potatoes are cooked through but not too soft. Drain the water and set aside. In a small sauté pan, melt the butter and then add the cooked carrots and potatoes and cook on medium-high for about 5 minutes, mixing often. Add the cream, and cook for another minute. Add the fresh herbs, mix well, season with salt and pepper, and serve.

Baked Artichoke Chicken with Chunky Potato, Spinach, and Zucchini Mash and Shallot and White Wine Cream Sauce

For the chicken:

    4 med. to large chicken thighs, bone in, skin on
    8 artichoke quarters in olive oil, cut in thin slices
    ½ cup panko breadcrumbs
    1 tbsp dried parsley
    3 tbsp olive oil
    Butter
    2 tbsp white wine
    Pinch of salt

Preheat oven to 375. Pat the chicken dry with paper towels, season with salt, and then using your fingers, lift the skin without removing it, and arrange the artichoke slices on the chicken, evenly between the 4 thighs. Pull the skin back over the artichokes, and set them aside. In a large saucepan, heat up 2 tablespoons of olive oil and 1 tablespoon of butter until hot but not smoking. Add the chicken skin side down, careful not to lose the artichokes, and sauté for 2 minutes on medium-high heat. Turn and sauté for another 2 minutes. Remove the chicken from the pan and set the pan aside. In a deep, medium-sized

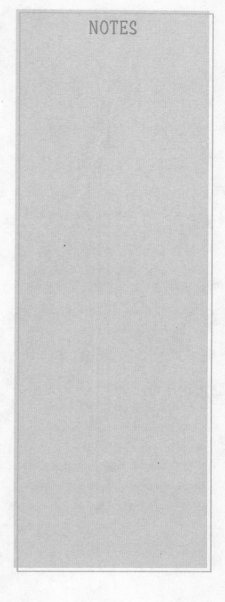

NOTES

NOTES

baking dish with a lid, add the breadcrumbs, parsley, 1 tablespoon of olive oil, and 2 tablespoons of wine, and salt. Mix together until it forms a paste. Spread the paste evenly on the bottom of the dish. Set the chicken skin side up on top of the paste; cover and bake at 375 for 25 minutes. Remove the lid, and then bake for another 7 minutes. Serve hot with the potato mash and white wine cream sauce.

For the wine sauce:
½ large Spanish or Vidalia onion, finely diced
1 large leek, white and light green parts only, finely diced
1 large shallot, finely diced
1 bunch green onions, finely chopped
4 garlic cloves, minced
2 tbsp chopped chives
1 cup white wine
½ cup cream
1 tbsp butter

On medium to high heat, add 2 tablespoons of butter and 1 tablespoon of olive oil to the pan the chicken cooked in. Heat until hot but not smoking then add the onions, leeks, and shallots, and cook until translucent. Add the garlic, and cook for one more minute. Add the wine and scrape all the bits from the bottom of the pan. Cook until the wine is almost completely evaporated. Add the green onions, and cook for about 1 minute. Add the cream, and cook together for another 2 minutes. Turn off the heat, add the butter and chives, and mix to incorporate. Serve on top of the chicken.

For the potato mash:
- 8 med red potatoes, skins on, cut in cubes
- 1 leek, white and light green part only, chopped
- 1 large shallot, chopped
- 6 garlic cloves, chopped
- 2 med zucchini squash, cut in small cubes
- 2 cups chopped spinach
- 3 heaping tbsp sour cream
- 2 tbsp chopped chives
- 1/3 cup milk
- ½ cup white wine
- 2 tbsp olive oil
- 3 tbsp butter

In a large saucepan, add the cubed potatoes, cover with cold water, and cook on high heat until the potatoes are tender. Meanwhile, add 2 tablespoons of olive oil and 1 tablespoon of butter to a sauté pan, and heat on medium-high heat until hot but not smoking. Add the leeks and shallots, and sauté until translucent. Add the garlic and

NOTES

123

Laura Laird

NOTES

zucchini, and cook together for about 2 to 3 minutes. Add the wine, and cook until the wine is completely evaporated. Allow the mixture to cool; then add it to a food processor along with the spinach and puree until smooth. After the potatoes are cooked, mash them until they are broken and smooth but still somewhat chunky; add the sour cream, milk, veggie puree, and mix together until incorporated. Add 2 tablespoons of butter and the chives, mix to incorporate, and serve hot with the chicken.

Chicken with Mushrooms and Zucchini

5 skinless, boneless chicken thighs

1 large red onion, diced

1 large shallot, diced

6 garlic cloves, minced

2 large jalapeno peppers, chopped

8-10 medium to large crimini (mini portabella) mushrooms, cut in small cubes

3 large zucchini cut in small cubes

8 asparagus stalks, sliced in ½ inch slices

1 ½ cups chopped fresh spinach

1 cup chopped fresh parsley

1 ½ cups white wine

3 tbsp heavy cream, warm

The juice of ½ lemon

Salt and pepper to taste

1 tbsp dried dill

2 tbsp dried parsley

1 tbsp granulated garlic

½ tbsp butter, soft

2 tsp flour

Olive oil

Butter

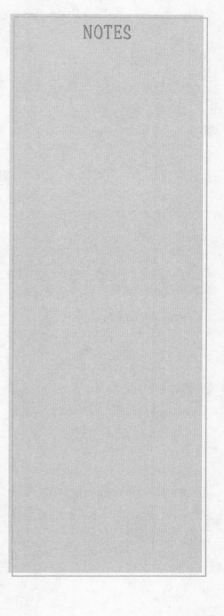

NOTES

In a small plate or bowl, mix together the softened butter and flour. Set aside. Pat the chicken thighs dry with

125

a paper towel, and season with salt and pepper. Add 2 tablespoons of olive oil to a large sauté pan set on medium-high heat. Heat the oil until hot but not smoking. Add the chicken thighs to the pan, and sauté until browned, about 2 minutes per side. Remove, cut each piece in 2, set them aside, and cover to keep them warm. To the same pan add 1 tablespoon of olive oil and 1 tablespoon of butter then add the onions, shallots, and jalapenos, and sauté mixing often on medium heat until the onion is translucent, about 5 to 7 minutes. Add the mushrooms, and sauté about another 5 minutes, mixing often. Season with salt and pepper, add the wine, and season with the dried herbs and granulated garlic. Mix well, add the chicken back to the pan, and bring to a boil. Turn the heat down to low, cover, and simmer gently for 7 minutes. After 7 minutes, add the zucchini and asparagus to the pan. Season again, mix well, cover, and simmer for an additional 10 minutes. Remove the cover and the chicken from the pan, and add the warm cream. Mix in; then add the flour and butter mixture. The sauce will start to thicken right away. Add the chopped spinach and the chicken back in, cover, and simmer for another 5 minutes. Remove from the heat, add the lemon juice and parsley, and mix well. Check for seasoning and serve hot.

Zucchini Stuffed with Turkey Sausage

3 zucchini, halved lengthwise

5 or 6 turkey bratwurst sausage, skin removed and
   broken in bite-size pieces

6 slices bacon, chopped

1 red onion, finely diced

6 garlic cloves, minced

1 cup chopped spinach

½ cup grated fresh mozzarella cheese

½ cup grated Parmesan cheese

Salt and pepper to taste

Preheat oven to 400 degrees. Season the zucchini halves with salt and pepper, and set them aside. Place a sauté pan on medium to high heat. When hot, add the bacon, and cook until crisp. Remove the bacon, and set it aside. Pour out of the pan all but 1 tablespoon of bacon grease, add 1 tablespoon of butter and the onion, and cook until soft, about 5 to 7 minutes. Add the garlic, and cook for another minute. Add the sausage, and cook for another 5 to 7 minutes, mixing often. Add the spinach, season with salt and pepper, and cook until the spinach is wilted. Remove from the heat, and add the grated mozzarella. Let the mixture cool for a few minutes. Fill each zucchini half with some of the mixture, and sprinkle them with some

NOTES

From the author:

Put the mozzarella in the freezer for about 10 minutes before using. It makes it easier to grate.

Laura Laird

NOTES

Parmesan cheese. Bake in the preheated oven for about 10 to 12 minutes until the zucchini is softened but still has a bite.

Turkey Italian Sausage with Onion, Leek, Bell Pepper, and Mushroom Sauce over Roasted Eggplant

1 large eggplant, sliced in thick rounds

6 fresh Italian sausage links, sliced on the bias in ½ inch slices

1 large sweet onion, diced

1 large leek, white and light green parts only, diced

1 large red bell pepper, quartered and sliced

1 large orange bell pepper, quartered and sliced

6 fresh garlic cloves, minced

12 to 14 med white cap mushrooms, sliced

½ cup red wine

½ cup chicken broth

1 tbsp flour

2 tbsp butter

4 tbsp half and half, warm

1 cup chopped fresh parsley

Olive oil

½ tsp cayenne pepper

Salt and pepper

1 tbsp dried parsley

½ tbsp dried basil

½ tbsp dried thyme

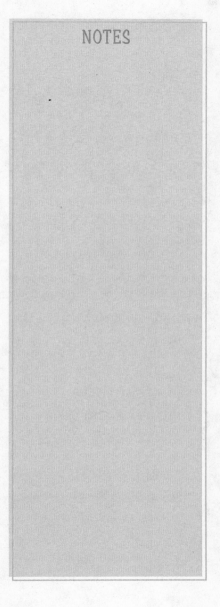

NOTES

NOTES

Preheat oven to 425 degrees. Season the eggplant with salt, and brush on both sides with olive oil mixed with 1 teaspoon of garlic powder and dried parsley. Place in one layer on a sheet pan and roast in the oven for 25 minutes. Turn the oven off and leave the eggplant in the oven until ready to use. In a large sauté pan, heat 3 tablespoons of olive oil until hot but not smoking. Cook the sausage slices about 1 to 3 minutes per side on medium-high heat until browned. Do not crowd the pan! Cook in 2 batches if necessary. After all the sausage is cooked, place them on a plate and set aside. Turn the heat to medium, and to the same pan add 1 tablespoon of butter and 1 tablespoon of olive oil. Add the mushrooms and brown for a couple of minutes. Add the bell peppers, leeks, and onion; season with salt and pepper, and cook together until soft and lightly browned. Sprinkle the flour, and mix together. Add the wine and broth, and mix until completely incorporated, making sure to scrape all the bits of flavor off the bottom of the pan. The sauce will start to thicken right away. Season with cayenne pepper and the dried herbs. Reduce heat to low, add the minced garlic, add the sausage back in, mix, cover the pan, and cook together for about 5 to 6 minutes. Add the cream, and cook for another couple of minutes. Check for seasoning, turn off the heat, add the fresh parsley, and mix together. Remove from the heat and cover. Let it sit for a few minutes. Serve in a large bowl on top of the eggplant slices.

Turkey Ragu with Orzo

1 cup orzo

6 slices bacon, chopped

6-turkey bratwurst sausage, skin removed and broken
    in bite-size pieces

½ lb ground turkey

1 large red onion, finely diced

2 leeks, white and light green parts only, finely diced

6 large garlic cloves, minced

10 white cap mushrooms, peeled and sliced

2 cups chopped kale

2 cups chopped spinach

1 cup white wine, room temp

1 14.5 oz can diced tomatoes

2 tbsp tomato paste

¼ cup cream, warm

1 cup minced fresh parsley

2 tbsp lemon juice

1 tbsp dried dill

1 tbsp dried parsley

Olive oil

Butter

Salt and pepper to taste

NOTES

In a very large sauté pan or Dutch oven set on medium to high heat, cook the bacon until crispy. Remove and set aside.

NOTES

Pour out of the pan all but 1 tablespoon of bacon grease, add 1 tablespoon of butter, and then add the onions and leeks and cook until translucent, about 5 to 7 minutes. Add the garlic, and cook for another minute. Add the sausage and ground turkey, season with salt and pepper, and cook together, mixing often, for about 7 minutes. Add the wine and dried parsley and dill, bring to a boil, lower the heat, and cook until the wine evaporates. In the meantime, cook the orzo according to the package directions and sauté the sliced mushrooms in 3 tablespoons of butter until browned. Season the mushrooms with salt and set aside. To the pan with the turkey, add the diced tomatoes and the tomato paste, and mix well to incorporate. Add the spinach and kale, mix, cover, and cook for about 5 to 7 minutes. Take the cover off, mix, season with salt and pepper, and add the warm cream. Add the bacon, cooked mushrooms, and orzo along with about a small ladle of the pasta water, and mix to incorporate. Cook for 5 minutes. Remove from the heat, add the lemon juice and fresh parsley mix, and serve.

Grilled Marinated Salmon
with Veggie Pasta

Marinade:

    ¼ cup olive oil

    2 tbsp balsamic vinegar

    2 tbsp red wine

    2 tbsp Worcestershire sauce

    1 tsp country Dijon mustard

    1 garlic clove, grated

    2 tbsp dried parsley

    2 tbsp dill

    1 tsp salt and 1 tsp pepper

Shake all ingredients together until very well incorporated.

    2 half lb each pieces of wild salmon, skin on

    1 small package linguine pasta, cooked according to
        the directions on the package

    1 red onion, diced

    6 garlic cloves, minced

    1 cup green peas

    6 crimini mushrooms, sliced

    8 sun-dried tomatoes in oil, sliced

    2 tbsp cream, warm

    1 cup chopped fresh parsley

    2 tbsp lemon juice

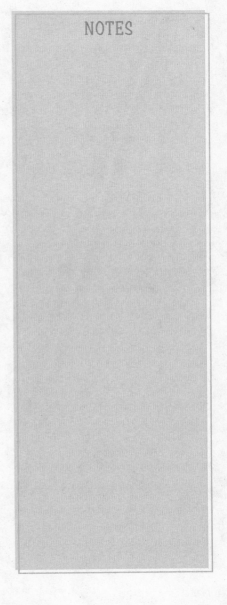

NOTES

133

NOTES

2 garlic cloves, grated
½ cup grated Parmesan cheese
Olive oil
Butter
Salt and pepper to taste

Place salmon pieces in a Ziploc bag, pour the marinade inside the bag enough to cover the salmon, close the bag, and refrigerate overnight. Remove the salmon from the marinade, and pat it dry. Add 2 tablespoons of olive oil to a sauté pan on medium heat, and cook the salmon for 4 minutes per side. Remove the salmon, and to the same sauté pan add 1 tablespoon of olive oil and 2 tablespoons of butter; add the red onion, and cook until translucent. Add the garlic, and cook for another minute. Add another tablespoon of butter; then add the peas, mushrooms, and sun-dried tomatoes; season with salt and pepper, and cook for about 7 minutes. Remove the pasta from the water, drain well, and then add the pasta to the vegetables in the sauté pan. Cook together for about 3 to 4 minutes, then add the cream, and cook for an additional 2 to 3 minutes, mixing well. Remove from the heat, add the parsley, lemon juice, and grated garlic; mix well and set aside covered to keep warm. Transfer the salmon to a cutting board, remove the skin, and using a fork (the salmon will be very tender) shred the salmon into bite-size pieces. Uncover the pasta, and add grated Parmesan cheese. Mix to incorporate, plate the pasta, and add the salmon on top. Sprinkle with some fresh parsley, and enjoy!

Baked Pasta with Shrimp and Béchamel Sauce

16 oz rigatoni or elbow pasta
20 uncooked shrimp, peeled and de-veined
½ red onion, diced
6 small garlic cloves, minced
12 yellow cherry tomatoes, halved
12 red cherry tomatoes, halved
¼ cup crumbled feta cheese
¾ cup minced fresh parsley
½ cup minced fresh cilantro
1 cup chopped fresh spinach
Olive oil
Butter
Salt and pepper

Béchamel sauce:
    2 tbsp butter
    2 tbsp flour
    1¼ cups milk, hot
    ¼ tsp nutmeg
    ¼ tbsp grated Parmesan cheese

Preheat oven to 400 degrees. Cook the pasta according to the package directions. Heat 1 tablespoon of butter

NOTES

135

Laura Laird

NOTES

and 1 tablespoon of olive oil in a medium-sized sauté pan until hot. Add the onion and garlic, and sauté until starting to brown. Add the tomatoes, season with salt and pepper to taste, and sauté for 2 or 3 minutes. Add the shrimp, and cook until lightly pink. Add the cooked pasta and 1 small ladle of pasta water, season, and cook together for just a few minutes. Add the parsley, cilantro, spinach, and feta cheese; mix well, and cook for 2 minutes. Add the béchamel sauce, mix, and bake in the preheated 400-degree oven for 12 minutes.

Halibut Pockets

2 large halibut stakes, about 1 ½ to 2 inches thick

2 med size shallots, finely sliced

2 cloves of garlic, finely sliced

6 thin lemon slices

6 slices butter

6 medium fresh basil leaves

4 sprigs fresh parsley

2 tbsp olive oil

Salt and pepper to taste

2 large aluminum foil squares

Preheat oven to 375. Prepare the pockets as follows: Place the aluminum foil on work surface. Spray lightly with cooking spray or brush lightly with olive oil. Place the halibut skin side down in the middle of the foil. Season with salt and pepper; then place 3 slices of butter followed by 6 slices of shallot, garlic, and 3 slices of lemon. Top with 3 basil leaves and 2 sprigs of fresh parsley. Drizzle lightly with 1 tablespoon of olive oil and a sprinkle of salt. Close the packet tightly. Repeat for the second halibut steak. Place the halibut packets on a small sheet pan, and bake for 25 minutes. Allow the halibut to rest in the oven with the heat turned off for another 10 minutes.

NOTES

From the author:

I find that a strong side dish can overwhelm the delicate taste of halibut, so I serve it with saffron jasmine rice, an equally delicate side dish.

NOTES

Saffron Jasmine Rice

1 cup jasmine rice
¼ white onion, finely chopped
1 small shallot, thinly sliced
4 garlic cloves, minced
½ tsp saffron
1 ½ cups chicken broth, warm
1 tbsp minced fresh dill
1 tbsp minced fresh basil
2 tbsp half and half or cream
2 tbsp lemon juice
Olive oil
Butter

Fill a small water glass about a quarter of the way with water. Add the saffron, and set it aside. In a large saucepan, heat 2 tablespoons of olive oil and 1 tablespoon of butter on medium-high heat. Add the white onion, and sauté until semi soft, about 2 minutes. Add the rice, and sauté together for another 2 minutes. Add the minced garlic and the sliced shallot, and sauté another 2 to 3 minutes. Season with salt and pepper to taste, then add the chicken stock and the saffron water and bring it to a boil. Reduce to a simmer, cover, and cook according to package directions, about 20 minutes. When the rice is done, add the cream, 1 tablespoon of butter, lemon juice, and fresh herbs, and mix together gently with a fork. Serve with the halibut.

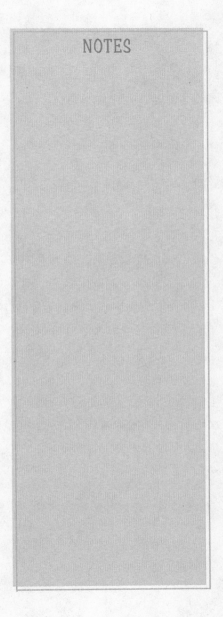

NOTES

Shrimp and Chicken Angel Hair Pasta with White Wine and Lemon-Butter Sauce

4 med size boneless, skinless ck thighs

16 med-large uncooked shrimp, peeled and de-veined, halved

2 med shallots, thinly sliced

4 large garlic cloves, minced

½ cup sun dried tomatoes in olive oil, sliced

1 cup thinly sliced spinach

1 cup chopped fresh parsley

Juice of 1 small lemon

1 cup white wine

1 tbsp butter

1 tbsp each dried parsley and basil

¼ tsp cayenne pepper

Salt

Olive oil

3 tbsp olive oil from the sun dried tomatoes

½ cup grated Parmesan cheese

8 oz (½ package) angel hair pasta

Cook the pasta according to the package directions, and set it aside. In a large sauté pan, heat up 1 tablespoon of olive oil until hot but not burning. Add the whole chicken thighs, and sear on both sides for about 3 minutes each side until golden brown. Remove and set aside. In the same pan, add 2 additional tablespoons of olive oil; then add the shallots, and cook slowly on medium low until soft. In the meantime, slice the chicken thighs in cubes. Add to the pan when the shallots are slightly browned. Increase heat to medium, and cook together for about a minute. Add the garlic, and cook for 1 minute. Add the wine, dry herbs, and cayenne pepper, and cook until the sauce has reduced slightly. Add salt and pepper to taste, then add the sun-dried tomatoes. Mix together, and add 1 tablespoon of the sun-dried tomatoes oil. Add the shrimp and the butter, and cook together for 1 minute. Add the spinach, and mix well. Add the pasta, remaining tablespoon of sun-dried tomatoes olive oil, and the fresh parsley; mix all of the ingredients together well. Add the lemon juice, and mix again. Sprinkle in the cheese, mix well, and let it rest for about a minute before serving.

NOTES

On the Side, Please: Side Dishes That Go Well with Anything

Oven-Roasted Asparagus

1 lb asparagus spears
2 to 4 tbsp olive oil
Salt and pepper to taste

Preheat oven to 400 degrees. Cut the ends off the asparagus; spread them on a large sheet pan in one layer. Pour the olive oil all over the asparagus, season with salt and pepper, and mix to coat. Roast in the oven 10 to 15 minutes.

NOTES

NOTES

Pan-Roasted Asparagus

10 to 14 asparagus spears
2 tbsp butter
¼ cup white wine
Salt and pepper to taste

Heat the butter in a medium-sized sauté pan. Add the asparagus, season with salt and pepper, and cook for about 3 to 5 minutes. Add the white wine, and cook until the wine is evaporated.

Oven-Roasted Brussels sprouts

1 lb Brussels sprouts
2 to 4 tbsp olive oil
Salt and pepper to taste

Remove the outer leaves from the Brussels sprouts and cut off the hard end. Cook the same as oven-roasted asparagus except for a total of 20 to 25 minutes

Oven-Roasted Garlic Potatoes

2 lb medium size new red potatoes, halved
1 cup fresh garlic cloves, slightly smashed and peeled
½ cup olive oil
2 tbsp dried parsley
2 tbsp dried dill
½ cup chopped parsley
¼ cup freshly grated Parmesan cheese
Salt and pepper to taste

Preheat the oven to 400 degrees. To a large bowl, add the potatoes, garlic cloves, dried parsley and dill, olive oil, and salt and pepper to taste. Mix together well until the potatoes are well coated with the oil, spices, and seasoning. Add the potatoes to a shallow, oven-proof baking dish in a single layer, and roast them in the preheated oven until the potatoes are golden brown, about 20 to 25 minutes. Remove from the oven, and sprinkle them with fresh chopped parsley and some Parmesan cheese.

NOTES

145

Ratatouille

1 small yellow onion, quartered and sliced

½ lg red onion, halved and sliced

6 fresh garlic cloves, minced

1 large green bell pepper, quartered and sliced

1 large tomato, quartered, seeded then sliced

1 can diced tomatoes

1 medium eggplant, peel on, sliced in ½ inch rounds

1 large zucchini, partially peeled and sliced on the bias in ½ inch rounds

4 med-sized potatoes peeled then sliced in ¼ inch rounds

1/3 cup heavy cream

1/3 cup white wine

1 cup finely chopped fresh parsley

Olive oil

Salt

2 tbsp dried parsley

1 tbsp dried oregano

1 tbsp dried basil

¼ tsp Cayenne pepper

Preheat oven to 400 degrees. In a large sauté pan, heat about ¼ inch of olive oil until hot. Brown the potato, eggplant, and zucchini slices in single layers until golden brown on both sides. Line a large sheet pan with some paper towels, place a rack on top, and gently remove all the cooked vegetables to the rack to drain. Pour out of the pan all but about 1 tablespoon of olive oil then add 1 tablespoon of butter, the onions and bell peppers, and cook on medium heat until translucent. Add the garlic, and cook for another minute. Season with salt and pepper, and add the tomato slices, cover, and cook for about 5 minutes. Remove the cover; add the diced tomatoes, 2 tablespoons of fresh parsley, and season with the dried herbs and cayenne pepper. Cook for 2 minutes then add the white wine and cook until the wine is reduced. Add the cream and cook together until the sauce coats the back of a wooden spoon. Remove from the heat, and set it aside. Spray a large, ovenproof baking dish with cooking spray; add half of the onion, bell pepper mixture, and spread it evenly on the bottom of the dish. Sprinkle with 2 tablespoons of fresh parsley. Start layering all the vegetable slices, overlapping each other. Add all but 2 tablespoons of the remaining fresh parsley. Pour the rest of the onion, bell pepper mixture on top, and sprinkle with the remaining fresh parsley. Cover, then place in the preheated 400-degree oven and bake for 20 minutes. Remove the cover, and bake for another 10 minutes. When done, remove from the oven and let the ratatouille rest for about 10 minutes, covered. Serve with a sprinkle of fresh parsley and Parmesan cheese.

NOTES

From the author:

Here's a less complicated version of this. Prepare the tomato and bell pepper sauce the same. Cut the eggplant, zucchini, and potatoes in large chunks. Brown the potatoes in olive oil and butter for 2 to 3 minutes, mixing often. Add the eggplant and zucchini, and sauté together for about 5 to 7 minutes. Season with salt and pepper and assemble the same as above and bake.

NOTES

Baked Cheese Cauliflower

1 cauliflower head, florets pulled
2 tbsp whipped cream cheese
2 tbsp heavy cream
¼ cup half-and-half
1 cup freshly grated Parmesan cheese
3 tbsp white wine
1 tsp fresh parsley
1 tsp fresh dill
Salt and pepper to taste

Preheat oven to 400. Fill a large pot with water, and bring it to a boil. Add salt and the cauliflower florets, and blanch for 5 minutes until semi-soft. Meanwhile fill a large bowl with cold water and ice and set it aside. After 5 minutes remove the cauliflower from the pot, and immediately transfer it to the ice water in the bowl to stop the cooking process. Remove the cauliflower from the bowl and set it aside on some paper towels to drain. In a small food processor, add the cream cheese, heavy cream, half-and-half, wine, parsley, and dill. Season with salt and pepper, and process until smooth. Add 2 tablespoons of Parmesan cheese and mix well. Lightly oil a shallow backing dish then add about 2 tablespoons of the cream mixture on the bottom and spread well. Arrange the cauliflower in one layer in the baking dish, and season with salt and pepper. Pour the rest of the cream mixture on top making sure that all the cauliflower florets are covered. Sprinkle the remaining Parmesan cheese on top, place in the preheated oven and bake until browned, about 20 to 25 minutes. Serve hot.

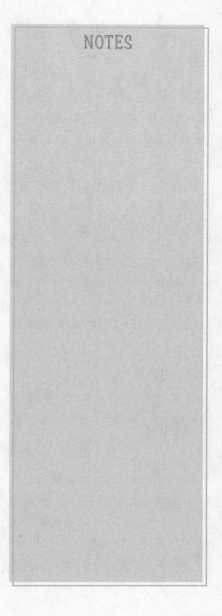

NOTES

Crab-Stuffed Mushrooms

12 medium white cap mushrooms + 4 for the stuffing,
  stems removed and peeled
1 10 ounce can crab meat
½ red onion finely diced
6 garlic cloves finely diced
2 tbsp country Dijon mustard
2 to 3 tbsp white wine
2 to 3 tbsp cream
½ cup finely chopped fresh parsley
Olive oil
Butter

Preheat the oven to 375 degrees. Place the 12 mushrooms cup side up on a cookie sheet lined with parchment paper or aluminum foil. In each mushroom, place a small piece of butter, about the size of the tip of your knife. Set aside. Dice the remaining 4 mushrooms finely. Place a small pan on medium-high heat then add about 2 tablespoons of butter and 1 tablespoon of olive oil. Add the diced red onion, and cook until translucent. Add the diced mushrooms and garlic. Season with salt and pepper to taste, and cook until the liquid rendered by the mushrooms is evaporated. Add the wine and cream, and cook until all the liquid is cooked down. Remove from the heat, and set aside to cool. In a medium-sized bowl, add the crabmeat, mustard, fresh parsley and the mushroom, onion, and garlic mixture. Mix together well then fill the mushroom caps with about 2 tablespoons of the crab mixture for each cap. Lightly press down with your hand to make a dome shape of the crab mixture. Bake in the 375-degree oven until the tops start to brown, about 20 to 30 minutes.

NOTES

A Blank Canvas: Rice and Risotto

Rice is a staple for many countries, and because it does not have a very distinct flavor on its own, rice is a blank canvas that can be combined with all kinds of vegetables and spices to make some very yummy side dishes. Combined with vegetables and meats, rice can also make a meal on its own. There are more than forty thousand different varieties of rice worldwide, but only a few have a high enough quality to be acceptable for growing here in the US. The most common types of rice most of us are probably familiar with are white rice, brown rice and Arborio rice, which is primarily used in making risotto. The white and brown rice come in three lengths. Long grain, which is long and slender and the kernels stay separated when cooked. Medium grain, with kernels that are a little shorter and wider, and when cooked they are more moist and tender and have a greater tendency to cling together than the long grain. Short grain rice has a short, plump, almost round kernel. When cooked, short grains are soft and cling together. Brown rice actually does have a slightly distinct nutty flavor, a chewy texture, and the light-brown color comes from layers of bran, which are rich in minerals and vitamins, making brown rice better for you than white rice. The other major distinction between white and brown rice is that white rice usually takes anywhere from fifteen to twenty minutes to cook where the brown rice takes anywhere from thirty-five to fifty minutes to cook. As I said earlier, Arborio rice is used mostly in the making of risotto, which is a major staple in the Italian cuisine and is, in my opinion, one of the best dishes on the planet today. Here are some wonderful recipes for rice and risotto.

Parmesan White Rice with Lemon and Basil

1 cup white rice
1½ cups chicken broth
The zest of ½ lemon
The juice of ½ lemon
½ tbsp-dried basil
¼ cup chopped fresh basil
1 tbsp butter
2 tbsp cream, warm
¼ cup freshly grated Parmesan cheese
Salt and pepper to taste

Bring the rice, chicken broth, dried basil, and salt and pepper to a boil. Cover with a tight-fitting lid, reduce heat to low, and simmer according to the package directions, about 15 to 20 minutes. About halfway through the cooking time, uncover, quickly add the lemon zest to the rice, cover, and continue cooking. When the rice is ready, fluff gently with a fork. Add the butter, cream, lemon juice, cheese, and fresh basil and mix everything together gently with a fork. Check for seasoning, and serve as a side dish.

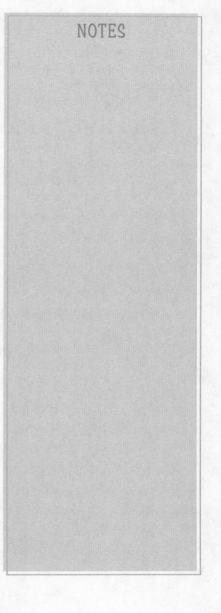

NOTES

Brown Rice with Spinach, Feta Cheese, Olives, and Parsley

NOTES

1½ cups brown rice
3 cups chicken broth
1 tbsp-dried parsley
1 cup chopped spinach
1 cup chopped fresh parsley
½ cup pitted kalamatta olives, chopped
½ cup crumbled feta cheese
2 tbsp olive oil
Salt and pepper to taste

Bring the rice, chicken broth, dried parsley, and salt and pepper to a boil. Cover, reduce the heat to low, and simmer according to the package directions, about 35 to 50 minutes. When the rice is cooked, fluff gently with a fork. Add the spinach, mix gently, and cover for 2 minutes. Remove the cover, add the olive oil, olives, parsley, and feta cheese; mix gently with a fork, check for seasoning, and serve as a side dish.

Brown Rice with
Fresh (Not Dried) Turkey Sausage

1½ cups brown rice

3½ cups vegetable broth, warm

2 small jalapeno pepper, seeds and veins removed
and finely chopped

1 small red onion, finely diced

3 large garlic cloves, minced

4 fresh turkey sausages, skin removed and broken in
small pieces

2 tsp dried oregano

½ tsp cayenne pepper

½ cup chopped fresh parsley

Olive oil

Butter

Salt and pepper to taste

In a medium-sized saucepan, heat 1 tablespoons of butter
and 2 tablespoons of olive oil on medium heat until hot but
not smoking. Add the onion and jalapeno peppers, and
cook about 5 minutes. Add the turkey sausage, season
with salt and pepper and cook for about 5 to 7 minutes
or until the sausage is starting to gently brown. Add the
garlic, and cook for another minute. Add the rice, and
cook together for 2 minutes. Add the vegetable broth,

NOTES

NOTES

dried oregano, and cayenne pepper; bring to a boil, cover, reduce the heat to low, and simmer about 40 to 45 minutes until the liquid is absorbed and the rice is cooked. Remove from the heat, fluff with a fork, and check for seasoning. Add 1 tablespoon of butter and the parsley, mix gently to incorporate and serve as a side dish or a meal in itself.

Shitake Mushrooms and Spinach Risotto

1 cup Arborio rice

1 cup white wine, room temp

3 cups chicken broth, heated

1 yellow onion, finely diced

4 large garlic cloves, minced

1 tbsp-dried parsley

½ tbsp-dried dill

1 lb shitake mushrooms, stems removed then sliced

1 cup chopped fresh spinach

½ cup chopped fresh dill

¾ cup grated Parmesan cheese

Olive oil

Butter

Salt and pepper to taste

Heat 3 tablespoons of butter and 1 tablespoon of olive oil in a medium-sized sauté pan. When hot, add the mushrooms and cook until browned, mixing often. When browned, season with salt and pepper, remove from the heat, and set aside. In a large sauté pan set on medium-high heat, melt together 2 tablespoons of butter and 2 tablespoons of olive oil. Add the onion, and sauté for about 2 to 3 minutes. Add the garlic, and sauté for another minute. Add the rice, season with salt and pepper, and

NOTES

NOTES

cook together for 3 to 5 minutes, mixing often. Reduce the heat down to low, add the white wine and the dried herbs, and cook until the wine evaporates, mixing often. Start adding the heated chicken broth, one ladle at the time, allowing the liquid to evaporate before you add the next ladle of broth. Repeat this process until all the broth is used. As it cooks, the rice starts to open up and release its starch, making the risotto creamy with the rice soft but with a slightly chewy center. With the last ladle of broth, add in the spinach. When the risotto is done, check for seasoning, add the cooked mushrooms, fresh dill, and cheese; mix to incorporate. Add 1 tablespoon of butter, mix, and serve.

Risotto Primavera

1 cup Arborio rice

1 cup white wine, room temp

3 cups vegetable broth, heated

1 red onion, finely diced

1 large leek, white and green parts only, finely diced

10 to 12 medium size shrimp, de-veined and halved long ways

6 to 8 large scallops, sliced

4 large garlic cloves, minced

1 small red bell pepper, diced

1 cup sliced asparagus, about ½ inch slices

1 cup chopped fresh spinach

½ tbsp dried thyme

1 cup chopped fresh parsley

¼ cup grated Pecorino Romano cheese

2 tbsp lemon juice

¼ cup cream

Olive oil

Butter

Salt and pepper to taste

Heat 1 tablespoon of butter and 1 tablespoon of olive oil in a medium-sized sauté pan over medium-high heat. Add the shrimp and scallops, and sauté for 2 minutes only,

NOTES

NOTES

From the author:

There are many ways in which you can cook risotto. Simple, with just some herbs and cheese; with spicy sausage, chicken, varied vegetables, even with steak, which can be precooked, cut in small chunks, and added at the end. The principal of cooking is the same for the rice itself, and usually, whatever flavor you whish to use, it should be added at the end.

mixing often. Season with salt and pepper, remove from the pan, and set aside. In the same sauté pan, add another tablespoon of butter, and sauté the red bell pepper and asparagus for 2 to 3 minutes. Season with salt and pepper, remove from the pan, and set aside. Place a large sauté pan on medium to high heat, and add 3 tablespoons of butter and 2 tablespoons of olive oil. Heat until hot but not smoking. Add the onions and leeks, and cook for 2 to 3 minutes. Add the garlic, and cook for another minute. Add the rice, season with salt and pepper, and cook together for 3 to 5 minutes, mixing often. Reduce the heat down to low, add the white wine and the dried thyme, and cook until the wine evaporates, mixing often. Start adding the heated vegetable broth, one ladle at the time, allowing the liquid to evaporate before you add the next ladle of broth. Repeat this process until all the broth is used. With the last ladle of broth, add in the cream, spinach, and the sautéed shrimp, scallops, bell pepper, and asparagus. When the risotto is done, check for seasoning; add the lemon juice, fresh parsley, and cheese, and mix to incorporate. Add 1 tablespoon of butter, mix, and serve.

But I'm Hungry Now!
A Few Starters to Make the Waiting Easier

It's always easier to get away with not having the dinner ready on time if you have something your guests can munch on while they wait. For those few occasions when the time got away from you, here are a few appetizer ideas.

Olive Spread

1 cup pitted kalamata olives

1 cup pitted green olives

2 garlic cloves, peeled

1-cup parsley

4 cherry tomatoes

¼ cup olive oil

1 tbsp mayonnaise

Salt and pepper

Add the first 5 ingredients to a food processor and pulse until coarsely chopped. Season with salt and pepper, add 1 tablespoon of mayonnaise, and start pulsing again while adding in the olive oil. Serve with pita chips or cucumber slices and celery for a lower calorie approach.

Cream Cheese Spread

16 oz whipped cream cheese, room temperature

1 small shallot peeled and quartered

3 roasted red bell peppers packed in water

½ cup chopped fresh basil leaves

½ cup chopped fresh dill

2 tbsp cream

1 tbsp Dijon mustard

Salt and pepper

Add the shallot, basil, dill, and mustard to a food processor and process until finely chopped. Add the roasted red bell peppers, and pulse a few times just to incorporate. Add the mix to the cream cheese along with the cream and some salt and pepper. Mix together to incorporate, and serve with celery sticks.

NOTES

NOTES

Guacamole

3 large ripe avocados, peeled, cored and cut in large
   cubes
2 garlic cloves, peeled
4 cherry tomatoes
½ cup fresh cilantro
½ cup fresh parsley
1 tsp lemon zest
1 tbsp lemon juice
1 tbsp mayonnaise
Salt and pepper

Chop the garlic, tomatoes, parsley, cilantro, lemon zest, lemon juice, and salt and pepper to taste in a food processor until everything forms a paste. Mash the avocados and mayonnaise together in a bowl with a fork or potato masher. Add the paste, mix in to incorporate, and serve with tortilla chips.

Stuffed Potatoes

6 fairly large Yukon gold potatoes, cleaned well and
   cut in half crosswise
1 lb cooked shrimp
6 green onions, tops removed and cut 3 times along
   the length of the onions
1 cup fresh parsley
¼ cup pitted kalamata olives
1 tbsp lemon juice
2 tbsp mayonnaise
Salt and pepper

Place the potatoes in a large pot, cover with cold water,
and bring to a boil. Lower the heat, and simmer until the
potatoes are fork tender but not too soft. When done,
remove the potatoes, put them in a colander, and rinse
with cold water. Set them aside to cool. In the meantime,
coarsely chop the shrimp, green onions, parsley, and olives
in a food processor. Transfer to a bowl, season with salt
and pepper, and mix in the lemon juice and mayonnaise.
When the potatoes are cooled, using the tip of a spoon,
very gently hallow out the middle of each potato half. The
whole should be large enough to hold about 2 tablespoons
of the shrimp mixture, but the sides should not be thin
enough to break. Serve sprinkled with a little fresh parsley.

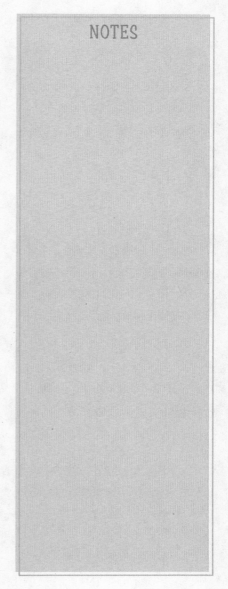

NOTES

167

Bruschetta

1 French baguette, sliced on the bias in 1 inch slices
2 garlic cloves
10 to 12 ¼-inch slices mozzarella cheese
20 to 24 tomato slices
10 to 12 large basil leaves
2 tbsp balsamic vinegar
2 tbsp finely minced fresh parsley
Olive oil
Salt and pepper

Preheat oven to 500 degrees. Lightly brush each baguette slice with olive oil, and season with salt and pepper on both sides. Place on a large sheet pan, and brown for about 2 or 3 minutes per side. Be careful not to burn the bread! In the meantime, add the tomato slices and basil leaves to a bowl, season with some salt and pepper, and add 2 tablespoons of balsamic vinegar and 4 tablespoons of olive oil. Gently mix together so that the tomatoes and basil are coated with vinegar and oil but they retain their shape. Remove the baguette slices from the oven, and rub the slices on one side with garlic while still warm. Assemble by topping each slice of bread with one slice of cheese, one basil leaf, and 2 overlapping tomato slices. Arrange on a platter, and sprinkle with a little fresh parsley.

Be Careful What You Pray For

Two for One: How My Husband and I Became Parents

In the first eight years of our married life, my husband and I moved six times. Twice in Houston, then from Houston to Corpus Christi, where we moved another two times, and finally from Corpus Christi to the Dallas/Fort Worth area, where we moved twice again! But when we bought our last house, we decided it was time to settle down and maybe hear the pitter-patter of little feet running around our new home. The problem was that by that time we had been married almost nine years, and in all that time we hadn't gotten pregnant once. We were hopeful for many years, but finally we decided to go a different route and adopt. There are many ways in which a family can adopt: open-ended adoptions, overseas adoptions, and adoptions through the state. We chose the latter because we saw it as a great opportunity to give a child that may not have a bright future a chance to live a better life. The thing with state adoptions, which in our case meant adopting through the Texas Child Protective Services, is that there are no guarantees. You have to get certified through the state to become first a foster parent, and then you have to mention to the agency you work with that you want to be a foster to adopt family, since your intention is to adopt. But even that is not a guarantee that the baby you get will be the one you will keep. This is not a particularly easy thing to go through. The first baby we received in our home was a three-day-old little boy who unfortunately had some drugs in his system at birth. This meant that he went through what could be characterized as withdrawals. He cried—hard—day and night, and so my first experience as a mother was a very difficult one. For the first two months, I think I slept maybe two or three hours a night at best. Finally, when he was two months old, this little boy began to transform. He smiled, he slept four or five hours during the night, he cried less, and it was obvious he had already stolen my heart. But then the call came, and we were told that someone in his mother's family wanted to take him. I've had some hardships in my life, and some were pretty hard, but this one was the hardest thing I ever had to do. How can anyone let go of a baby they've nurtured and seen through a very hard time? But I had to! Those are the rules with these kinds of adoptions, and there was nothing my husband and I could do. Even after he left, I prayed hard, believing, hoping, pleading that he would return. Finally, I realized I had to let go and believe that God had a plan and He would bring the right child into our home. A month later, He did! Her name was Faith, a three-day-old little girl who, because of the unusual circumstances of her mother's pregnancy, was completely healthy at birth! It took me a couple of days to bond with her because I was still grieving for the loss of my little boy, but my heart was opened to her in an instant one morning while I was watching her sleep, and I literally fell in love with her. The first couple of months of our relationship were the sweetest I had ever experienced. I would pick her up from her crib and lay her on my chest and sleep holding her! She was the best baby ever! We called her our "one waa" girl because she didn't cry! She would just say "one waa" and maybe fifteen minutes later another one, and she was smiling all the time. I didn't know how babies were supposed to act, but even I figured out that it was probably unusual for a baby to wake up with a smile, go to sleep with a smile, and always be happy, but that's how she was! Both my husband and I fell in love with her, and we had a blast. Then, three months later, our agency told us of another little girl that was just born and waiting at the hospital for her new family to pick her up. We decided we were going to be that family, and we went and got her. Her name: Grace! So now we had Faith and Grace, and this time we got to keep them both! When Grace was nine months old, we legally became her parents, and two months later when Faith was fourteen months old, we became her legal parents! The journey was hard but interesting, and, as time passed and we realized we would actually get to keep them both, we saw the divine hand in all of it. Usually parents don't choose their babies, and, most of the time, they don't choose when they become pregnant, but in this case, these little girls were handpicked for us! We chose them personally, and because of this realization, I started looking at adoption as a miracle, a way in which a couple can bless a child, but at the same time they themselves can be blessed so much more by the one they chose! Today my little girls are three years old, and they're not a handful; they are two huge handfuls! There are times when raising almost twins can get challenging, to say the least, but then I remember the plan, the divine intervention, the special way in which they came to me, and I know the One that has seen me through all my difficulties, the One that brought my husband and I together, the One that hand picked those little girls for me, will be the same One that will see me through my life as a parent! As Faith and Grace grew and started eating regular food, I noticed that Grace was a little picky with what she ate, but I became very happy when I noticed she ate everything I made! I make many things for them, but I want to talk about breakfast time because that is the time they spend with their daddy every morning. He makes them breakfast, and I want to write down some of the simple and yet very delicious things he makes for them.

Laura Laird

NOTES

Butter Eggs with Grated Cheese

4 eggs
2 tbsp butter
1 tbsp grated Parmesan or Pecorino Romano cheese

Heat the butter in a small saucepan on low heat until melted. Add the eggs, sunny-side up, and cook until the whites start to harden. Break the eggs with a small spatula, and serve with grated cheese on top. The eggs are moist and very tasty because of the butter and cheese.

Sausage Patties

½ small package bulk turkey breakfast sausage
2 tbsp olive oil
Salt

Heat the oil in a small saucepan on medium-high heat. Break the sausage in 4 parts, and flatten into round patties. Add the patties to the pan, and cook for 2 to 3 minutes per side, seasoning each side with a little salt. Add about 3 tablespoons of water to the pan, cover, and continue cooking until the water is evaporated.

NOTES

Laura Laird

NOTES

Fresh Strawberry-Banana Sauce

10 to 12 fresh strawberries cut in small pieces
1 large ripe banana sliced
4 tbsp or more honey

Place the strawberries, banana, and honey in a bowl, and puree until smooth with a hand blender fitted with a metal blade. Serve on toast or pancakes. For a different taste, add 2 tablespoons of chocolate sauce.

Let's Meet for a Cup of Java: Breakfast Food

I love making all kinds of food, but if someone asked me if I had a favorite, I would say it was breakfast! I love the yummy taste, the simplicity, the variety, and, of course, the coffee that comes with it. Over the years, I made all kinds of different versions of breakfast food, but it seems the staples are always, eggs, potatoes, and sausage or bacon. But this is here in the states. In my homeland, breakfast was a different story. In the city, we rarely had eggs and sausage, and we never had bacon. When I was in the country at my grandmother's house, eggs were the norm because she raised hens and turkeys, and we ate the eggs from both. I honestly don't remember eating better tasting eggs. Turkey eggs are about three times the size of a normal hen egg, and both types of eggs had whites with a consistency almost as gelatinous as jello and yolks that were tall, orange in color, and very thick. My grandmother would cook them sunny-side up and serve them with fresh bread made in the morning and a tall glass of hot milk, usually bought from a neighbor that had cows. It was heaven! My maternal grandmother loved to make me cheese omelets, and I loved eating them. Eggs beaten with fresh cheese and served with fresh tomatoes. Many times in the spring and summer, I would go to her house for breakfast. At my house, as unusual as it might sound, most of the time we had polenta for breakfast. We made it fresh and mixed it with eggs, sour cream, and butter when we had those things; when we didn't, we ate it with milk. Sometimes we would make this dish baked in the oven, and it was really delicious! Here's that recipe with a few personal tweaks, along with some of my own creations through the years.

NOTES

Baked Cheesy Polenta with Eggs and Sour Cream

1 cup corn meal
2½ cups vegetable broth
1 cup milk
1 cup crumbled feta cheese
4 eggs
½ cup sour cream
¼ cup grated pecorino Romano cheese
1 stick of butter divided in 16 pieces
Salt and pepper to taste

Preheat oven to 350 degrees. In a large saucepan, bring the vegetable broth, milk, and salt and pepper to taste to a boil. Reduce heat to low, and start adding the corn meal a little at the time, mixing continually. Simmer for 15 to 20 minutes until the polenta thickens, mixing often. Remove from the heat, and set aside. Spray the bottom of a large ovenproof dish with some cooking spray, and add 8 pieces of butter; spread evenly. Pour half of the cooked polenta over the butter, then sprinkle ½ cup feta cheese. Very carefully crack each egg over the cheese. Gently pour the rest of the polenta over the eggs, place the other 8 pieces of butter on top, and sprinkle the rest of the feta cheese. Spread the sour cream evenly over the feta, and sprinkle the top with the grated Parmesan. Bake in the preheated oven for about 20 minutes. Serve hot. This is a very delicious if not low-calorie meal best suited for cold, winter mornings.

NOTES

NOTES

Spinach, Mushroom, and Bacon Frittata

10 eggs, beaten

5 tbsp heavy cream

6 slices of bacon cooked crispy and crumbled

1 small yellow onion, finely diced

1 bunch (about 8 stocks) green onion, chopped

10 to 12 crimini (baby portabella) mushrooms, diced

2 cups chopped spinach

1 cup chopped fresh parsley

½ cup chopped fresh dill

½ cup grated Parmesan cheese

Salt and pepper to taste

Olive oil

Butter

Preheat oven to 350 degrees. In a large sauté pan, heat 2 tablespoons of butter and 1 tablespoon of olive oil until hot but not smoking. Add the yellow onions and mushrooms, season with salt and pepper, and cook until softened. In the meantime, in a large bowl mix together the eggs, heavy cream, bacon, green onions, spinach, parsley, dill, and parmesan cheese until well incorporated. Season with salt and pepper. Add the egg mixture to the cooked onions and mushrooms, and mix. Cook on low heat until the bottom sets, about 2 minutes. Place the pan in the preheated oven, and cook until the eggs set in the middle, about 15 to 20 minutes. Remove promptly. Do not over cook! Serve hot with a little sour cream.

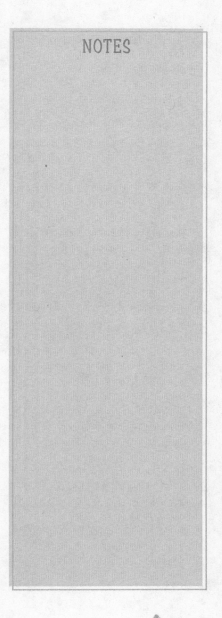

NOTES

Mexican Frittata

8 eggs, beaten

3 large roma tomatoes diced

3 garlic cloves, grated

4 tbsp heavy cream

½ cup Colby jack cheese or any Mexican cheese

½ tsp paprika

1½ tsp oregano

¼ tsp cayenne pepper

½ cup chopped fresh parsley

1 fresh jalapeno pepper, de-veined, seeded and chopped

½ red onion, diced

4 garlic cloves, minced

Olive oil and butter

Salt to taste

Preheat oven to 350. In a large sauté pan, heat up 1 tablespoon of butter and 2 to 3 tablespoons of olive oil, hot but not smoking. Add the diced onion and jalapeno pepper, and cook for 2 to 4 minutes until tender. Add the minced garlic, and cook for another 1 minute. In the meantime, beat the eggs and add the next 8 ingredients, mixing well. Pour the egg mixture into the pan with the cooked onion and jalapenos; mix, and cook until the bottom sets, 1 or 2 minutes. Place the pan in the preheated oven, and cook for 15 to 20 minutes until the eggs set in the middle. Do not overcook! When there are a few minutes of cooking left, sprinkle the top of the frittata with a little cheese. Remove promptly and serve.

NOTES

Scrambled Cheese and Spinach Eggs with Cheesy Hash Browns and Sausage Patties

8 eggs

3 tbsp cream

1 28 oz package raw Shredded Hash Browns

1 lb ground turkey

1½ red onion, finely diced

6 large garlic cloves, minced

2 large garlic cloves, grated

1 cup chopped fresh spinach

½ cup crumbled goat cheese

1 cup grated pecorino Romano cheese

1 tsp paprika

1 tsp allspice

1 cup chopped fresh parsley

1 cup chopped fresh dill

Olive oil

Butter

Salt and pepper to taste

In a large sauté pan set on medium-high heat, melt 2 tablespoons of olive oil and 1 tablespoon of butter until hot but not smoking. Add the onion, and sauté until translucent, about 3 to 5 minutes. Add the garlic, season with salt and pepper, and cook for another minute. Set aside about a third of the onion and garlic mixture to cool. Add another 2 tablespoons of olive oil and the shredded potatoes to the sauté pan, and mix to combine. Season with salt and pepper to taste, turn the heat down to medium, and allow the potatoes to cook, mixing often. In the meantime, add the ground turkey, 2 eggs, the grated garlic, 1 teaspoon of paprika, 1 teaspoon allspice, ½ a cup fresh parsley, ½ a cup fresh dill, salt and pepper to taste, and the reserved cooked onion and garlic mixture to a large bowl. Mix all ingredients gently with a fork to combine. Place a medium-sized sauté pan on medium-high heat and add 2 tablespoons of olive oil. Start making round sausage patties, about 1½ inches in diameter, turn the heat down to medium, and add them to the heated oil in the sauté pan in one layer at the time. If necessary, work in batches so you don't overcrowd the pan. Cook the sausage patties about 3 to 5 minutes per side on medium heat. While the sausage and potatoes are cooking, beat the remaining 6 eggs together with the cream. Mix in the crumbled goat cheese, ¼ cup pecorino Romano cheese, 1 tablespoon each of fresh parsley and dill and salt and pepper to taste. Place another medium-sized sauté pan on medium heat, add 1 tablespoon of olive oil and 2 tablespoons of butter and the chopped spinach. Sauté the spinach for about 2

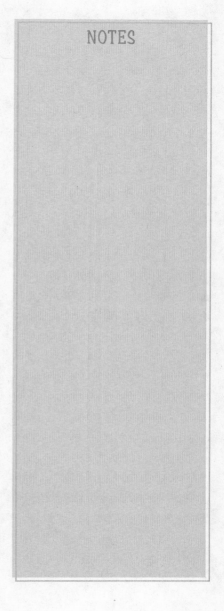

NOTES

NOTES

minutes until it begins to wilt. Turn the heat down to low, and add the scrambled egg mixture. Allow the eggs to set on the bottom then start very gently mixing the eggs with a spatula until they begin to set. Remove the eggs from the heat when they are still a little runny. The eggs will continue cooking in the pan for a few more minutes, making the finished product light and fluffy. Do not overcook the eggs. When the hash browns are done, take them off the heat, add in the remaining pecorino Romano cheese, mix it in, and allow them to sit covered for a couple of minutes. When everything is finished, serve some of the scrambled eggs with 2 or 3 sausage patties and some of the cheesy hash browns.

Baked Eggs with Cream Cheese and Fresh Dill

8 eggs
16 oz cream cheese, room temperature
½ cup cream
½ cup chopped fresh dill
½ cup grated Parmesan cheese
1 tsp cayenne pepper
Salt and pepper to taste

Preheat oven to 350 degrees. In a medium-sized bowl, mix together the cream cheese, fresh dill, and cayenne pepper. Season with salt and pepper, and put half of the mixture in a different bowl. Add the cream to the second bowl of cream cheese, and carefully mix to incorporate. Spray 4 medium size ramekins with some cooking spray. Divide the cream cheese from the first bowl equally between the ramekins, about 2 tablespoons per ramekin. Very gently crack 2 eggs in each ramekin, and top with the cream cheese and cream mixture from the second bowl, equally dividing the mixture between the 4 ramekins. Top each ramekin with some Parmesan cheese, and bake the eggs in the preheated oven for about 20 to 30 minutes. Serve hot.

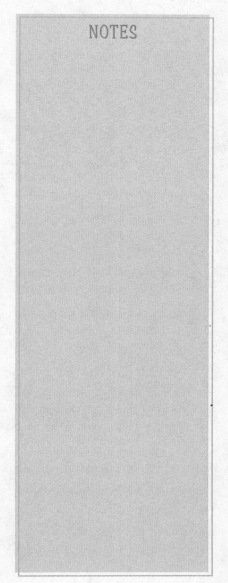

NOTES

Avocado Cream Sauce

1 cup + 2 tbsp heavy cream or half-and-half
½ cup grated Parmesan cheese
½ ripe avocado
Salt and pepper to taste

Smash the avocado, 2 tablespoons of cream, and 1 teaspoon of salt in a bowl until very smooth. Heat the cream on medium-low heat in small saucepan until it starts to simmer. Take off the heat, and gently start to whisk in the Parmesan cheese. When the sauce starts to thicken, whisk in the avocado mixture. Season with salt and pepper and serve.

I believe one of the reasons I love breakfast time so much is because it comes with coffee. I am the type of person who cannot sleep if I drink coffee after about 1 p.m., so I really enjoy my 1 or 2 cups of coffee in the morning. But I don't like black coffee, so I really like to dress it up. Usually I just add some kind of sweetener and some fat-free milk, but if I am in an indulgent mood, I make a little richer. Here are a couple of ideas you might like.

For a 16 oz coffee mug:

Chocolate Dream

NOTES

12 oz freshly brewed hot coffee

2 tbsp chocolate ice cream

2 tbsp half-and-half

2 tbsp Kahlua coffee liquor

2 tsp sugar or 1 pkg sweetener

2 tbsp whipped cream

2 tsp chocolate sauce

Add the ice cream, half-and-half, Kahlua, and sweetener to the coffee mug, pour the hot coffee over, and mix gently. Mix the whipped cream and chocolate sauce and add it to the coffee.

NOTES

Irish Vanilla

12 oz freshly brewed hot coffee
2 tbsp vanilla ice cream
2 tbsp half-and-half
2 tbsp Irish Cream
2 tsp sugar or 1 pkg sweetener
2 tbsp whipped cream

Add the ice cream, half-and-half, Irish Cream, and sweetener to the coffee mug, pour the hot coffee over, and mix gently. Top with whipped cream.

As you might have guessed by now, I am not big on baking, but I do love pastries. For a simple breakfast, enjoy these coffees with some fresh croissants or a fruit muffin.

There Is Nothing Like a Romantic Date Night: Recipes for a Special Occasion

My husband and I always enjoy a date night. These days though, with two little ones running around, date nights don't happen as often as they should anymore. But we still do get away sometimes, and we really love going to a movie, a play, or a concert, and then to a nice restaurant for a romantic meal for two. Sometimes my husband just takes the girls to a friend's house, and I stay behind and cook a romantic meal for us. Then we enjoy eating our food and drinking a glass of champagne in a quiet house. It's even more romantic, I think, because I get to cook something special for both of us, and I always love that! Here are a few recipes that I make as often as I can for occasions like our anniversary or Valentine's Day.

Rib Eye and Lobster Tower

2 rib eye rounds, 8 oz each

6 oz cooked lobster meat

1 small sweet potato, peeled and cubed

2 medium red potatoes, peeled and cubed

1 ½ cup chopped spinach

3 roasted garlic cloves, mashed

¼ cup + 2 tbsp finely chopped fresh parsley

¼ cup + 1 tbsp finely chopped fresh cilantro

4 tbsp lemon juice

½ cup port wine

1 cup heavy cream

2 tbsp sour cream

2 tbsp butter

5 tbsp butter, melted

Olive oil

Salt

2 tbsp freshly ground pepper

Take the steak out of the refrigerator, and keep to room temperature about 30 minutes before cooking. In the meantime, boil the potatoes until very tender. Gently heat the lobster meat in a small saucepan with a little olive oil. Do not overcook. Add 4 ounces of the warm lobster meat to a bowl, and add salt and pepper to taste, 2 tablespoons of lemon juice and 2 tablespoons of melted butter, and mix well. Set aside, keeping warm. Smash the boiled potatoes together with salt and pepper to taste, mashed roasted garlic, 2 tablespoons of melted butter, 2 tablespoons of sour cream, ¼ cup of cilantro, and ¼ cup of parsley. Set aside. Lightly wilt the spinach in a little olive oil then add a pinch of salt and 2 tablespoons of lemon juice. Set aside. Take the remaining 2-ounce lobster meat, and bring to a light simmer with ¼ cup of heavy cream, salt and pepper. Puree together in a food processor, and add 1 tablespoon of lemon juice. Puree again until very smooth. Set aside. Season the steak on both sides with salt then press one side into the ground pepper. Place a medium-sized sauté pan on medium-high heat, add 2 tablespoons of butter and 1 tablespoon of olive oil, and heat until very hot. Add the steaks, pepper side down, and cook 4 minutes per side for medium rare. Remove from the pan, and let the steaks rest, covered. To the same pan on medium heat, add the port and mix to scrape the bits off the bottom of the pan. Simmer for a few minutes until the port reduces by half. Add ¾ cup of heavy cream, and gently simmer until the sauce thickens slightly and coats the back of a wooden spoon. Season with salt to taste, and add 1 tablespoon of fresh parsley.

NOTES

NOTES

Assemble as follows:

Start in the middle of a white large plate, and pour 1 large tablespoon of the lobster sauce. Start making circles with the spoon in the sauce until the bottom circle of the plate is covered in sauce. Place a small metal circle form that has been sprayed inside with a little cooking spray in the middle of the plate, and fill about halfway with smashed potatoes. Gently press down the potatoes then gently remove the metal circle. Add half of the cooked spinach on top of the potatoes also in a circle. Add half of the lemon-and-butter-seasoned lobster meat on top of the spinach, also in a circle. Slice each steak in 5 slices, and arrange on top of the lobster meat like the petals of a flower. Spoon some of the port and cream sauce on top, and sprinkle the whole plate with finely chopped fresh parsley for decoration. Repeat with the second plate.

Grilled Red Snapper with Sautéed Mixed Vegetables and Champagne Saffron Lemon Sauce

2 red snapper filets, skin on, bones removed

½ white onion, finely chopped

1 med shallot, finely chopped

4 garlic cloves, minced

10 med shitake mushrooms, sliced

8 finger link potatoes sliced

½ Napa cabbage, sliced in half; then each half in half again length wise and thinly sliced

½ cup finely sliced fresh spinach

1 cup brut champagne

¼ cup chicken broth

½ cup heavy cream

Butter

The juice of 1 lemon

1 tsp saffron

1 tbsp dried dill

1 tbsp finely chopped parsley

Salt and pepper to taste

Season the fish with salt and pepper then brush with olive oil and sprinkle with dried dill. Add 2 tablespoons

NOTES

of olive oil to a sauté pan, and cook the fish on low to medium heat 5 to 7 minutes per side, depending on the size of the filets. When done, remove and cover to keep warm. In the same sauté pan, add 2 tablespoons of butter and 1 tablespoon of olive oil, and heat on medium-high heat until hot but not smoking. Add the mushrooms, and cook until browned. When browned, add the onions and shallots, and cook until slightly softened, season with salt and pepper to taste, and remove from the pan. To the same pan, add 1 tablespoon of butter and 1 tablespoon of olive oil; add the potatoes and cook until browned and slightly softened. Make sure not to soften too much. Season with salt and pepper, and remove from the pan. To the same pan, again add another tablespoon of olive oil then add the cabbage and the garlic, and cook until slightly browned and softened. Add back to the pan the mushrooms, onions, and potatoes, check for seasoning, mix together, and cook for about a minute; then add ½ a cup of the champagne. Cook until the champagne has totally evaporated. Add the spinach and 1 tablespoon of butter, remove from heat, mix together, and set aside. In a small saucepan, add the remaining ½ cup of champagne, and bring to a simmer. Cook for a couple of minutes, add the chicken broth and the saffron, and continue cooking until it's starting to reduce. Add the cream, and cook together gently until it thickens slightly and coats the back of a wooden spoon. Season to taste, remove from the heat, add the juice of ½ a lemon and 1 tablespoon of butter, and mix together gently until the butter is incorporated. Add 1 tablespoon of freshly chopped parsley.

To serve:

Spoon some of the sauce on the bottom of a plate. Gently add a mound of the vegetable mixture in the middle of the plate on top of the sauce, leaving about a half an inch of margin all around. Cut 2 pieces from the fish about 3 to 4 inches in length, and gently place 1 piece on top of the vegetable mound. Spoon a small amount of sauce on top of the fish; then squeeze some lemon juice over the whole thing. Repeat for the second plate.

NOTES

Merlot Risotto with Thyme, Mascarpone Cheese, and Shitake Mushrooms

1 cup Arborio rice
3 medium to large shallots, diced
2 cups merlot, room temp
1 ½ cups vegetable broth, warm
1 lb shitake mushrooms, stems removed and sliced
3 tbsp mascarpone cheese
2 tbsp cream
1 tbsp minced fresh thyme
1 tbsp fresh lemon juice
Butter
Olive oil
Salt and pepper to taste

Mix the mascarpone cheese and cream in a small bowl, add the thyme, mix in, and set aside. In a medium-sized sauté pan, melt 3 tablespoons of butter and 1 tablespoon of olive oil until hot. Add the sliced shitake mushrooms, and sauté until browned. Season with salt and pepper, mix in, and set aside. In a large sauté pan, heat 2 tablespoons of olive oil and 1 tablespoon of butter until hot. Add the shallots, and sauté until translucent. Add the Arborio rice, and sauté together for a couple of minutes mixing often. Season with salt and pepper, and add 1 cup of merlot. Turn the heat down to medium-low, and cook until all the wine evaporates, mixing often. Add the second cup of merlot, and cook the same way. Start ladling the vegetable broth, one ladle at the time, waiting until the liquid evaporates before adding the next ladle. Continue until all the liquid is incorporated. Check for seasoning, and add more salt and pepper if needed. Turn the heat off, and fold in the cooked mushrooms. When the mushrooms are well incorporated, gently fold in the mascarpone cheese, cream, and thyme mixture. Finish with the lemon juice and 1 tablespoon of butter. Serve right away.

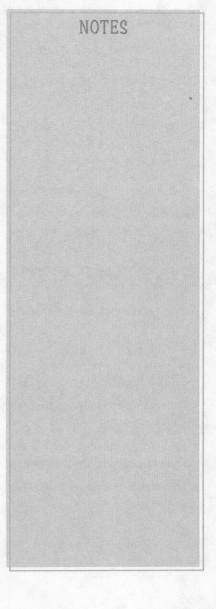

NOTES

NOTES

Cream of Artichoke Soup with Parsley and Crème Fresh

2 16 oz bags frozen artichoke hearts, defrosted
1 small white onion, quartered and sliced thick
2 garlic cloves, slightly smashed, skin on
2 cups vegetable broth, heated
½ cup heavy cream, warm
½ cup + 2 tbsp minced fresh parsley
Olive oil
Butter
Salt and pepper to taste

Preheat oven to 400 degrees. When the artichoke hearts are defrosted, pat them well with paper towels, place them on a rack placed inside a large sheet pan, and allow them to dry for a few minutes. Lift the rack, wipe away any liquid that has drained onto the sheet pan, place the artichokes, white onion, and garlic on the sheet pan, drizzle with about 2 tablespoons of olive oil season with salt and pepper to taste and roast in the preheated oven for about 20 minutes. Remove from the oven, and allow them to cool. Transfer the roasted artichokes, onion, and peeled garlic into a large food processor fitted with a metal blade, and puree until smooth. With the blade on, slowly drizzle in 1 cup of the vegetable broth. Add the soup to a saucepan on low heat, and start to slowly add the second cup of vegetable broth. Season with more salt and pepper if needed, and gently mix in the cream and 1 tablespoon of butter. Add ½ a cup minced parsley, and gently mix to incorporate. Serve hot with a dollop of crème fresh and a sprinkle of fresh parsley on top.

These Friends of Mine: My Closest Friends and the Foods They Like to Eat

There are many wonderful things about moving around a lot, but I think my favorite part is making friends everywhere we go. I love making friends, and I love cooking for them, so having lived in three different cities has opened the door for meeting quite a few interesting and wonderful people. When we bought our last house, I was working as a realtor, and through that job and through buying the house, we met Mike and Mary Evelyn Wallace, a couple who happens to have four children. At the time, I didn't have any children of my own, so our friendship started with me having the kids over for sleepovers and their parents over for dinner. Through the Wallaces, we met another great couple, John and Alicia Ceynar and their three children. It didn't take long for all of us to become friends and to find out that we all share the same faith in God and the same love for good food. It's fun when all of us get together, and I have to admit that one of the reasons I like them so much is because they make such a big deal about my food! One summer, the Wallaces left on vacation and some of their other friends decided to pull their resources and do a little remodeling of their home. When they came home from their vacation, they were quite surprised. My contribution: food, of course. I was in their home making chicken soup. It

201

went over pretty well since they were tired from the trip and hungry. But in all fairness, the Wallaces eat just about anything I put in front of them. My friend Alicia, though, is another story. She once joked that since she couldn't cook anything that had more than five ingredients, I had to come up with some special recipes for her. What I said was that since she seems to be allergic to just about any ingredient I cook with, that would be a monumental task. But, no matter what we eat or what reason for our gatherings, when we do get together, we all have a great time, which always reminds me what life really is all about: God, family, and good friends! Here are a few of my friends' favorite recipes.

Chunky Chicken Soup

1 cooked rotisserie chicken, meat removed and cut in
   cubes

2 quarts chicken broth, heated

1 cup white wine, room temperature

1 large red onion, chopped

6 large garlic cloves, minced

6 to 8 medium size Yukon gold or red potatoes, cubed

3 large carrots, peeled and cubed

10 to 12 medium-sized white cap mushrooms, peeled
   and cut in thick cubes

½ large red cabbage, sliced

2 cups chopped spinach

1 cup minced fresh parsley

¼ cup heavy cream, heated

2 tbsp balsamic vinegar

2 tbsp dried parsley

1 tsp cayenne pepper

Salt and pepper to taste

3 tbsp olive oil

3 tbsp butter

NOTES

In a large Dutch oven with tall sides placed on medium to
high heat, melt 1 tablespoon of butter with 3 tablespoons
of olive oil. Add the onions and carrots, and sauté for about

NOTES

5 minutes. Add the mushrooms and garlic, and sauté for another 5 minutes. Season with salt and pepper; add the wine, dried parsley, and cayenne pepper and bring to a boil. Add the chicken, and simmer for about 5 minutes. Add 1 quart of the chicken broth, and bring to a boil. Add the potatoes, and simmer for 5 minutes. Add the cabbage, and simmer for another 5 minutes. At this point, add more broth, if necessary. There should be enough to cover all the vegetables. Add the cream, and let it simmer for 2 or 3 minutes. Add the spinach, mix well, check for seasoning, and simmer for an additional 5 minutes. Remove from the heat, add the balsamic vinegar, 2 tablespoons of butter and the fresh parsley, mix well, and cover. Let the soup rest for 5 minutes before serving.

Steak and Spinach Risotto

4 6 oz rib eye steaks, about 1 inch thick

1½ cups Arborio rice

1 cup white wine, room temperature

4½ cups chicken broth, heated

1 red onion, diced

1 large leek, white and light green parts only, halved
   and sliced

6 garlic cloves, minced

½ 16 oz bag frozen peas

1 cup asparagus, sliced on the bias in ½ inch slices

1½ cups chopped spinach

¼ cup cream, warm

1 cup freshly grated Parmesan cheese

1 cup chopped fresh parsley

Olive oil

Butter

Salt and pepper

Heat 1 tablespoon of olive oil in a large sauté pan until hot. Season the steaks with salt and pepper, add them to the pan, and cook on medium-high heat about 4 minutes per side. Remove the steaks, cover, and set them aside. To the same pan, add 1 tablespoon of olive oil and 2 tablespoons of butter, then add the onions and leeks, and sauté until

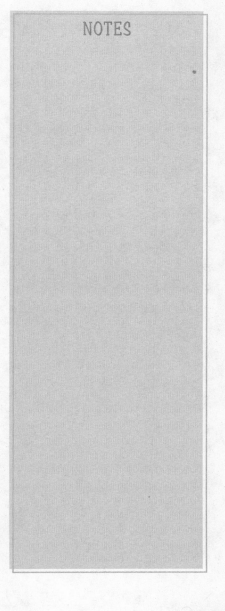

NOTES

NOTES

translucent. Add the garlic, and cook for another minute. Add the rice, season with salt and pepper, and cook together, mixing often for about 3 minutes. Add the wine, mix, turn the heat down to medium-low, and cook until the wine is absorbed. Start adding the heated chicken broth, one ladle at the time, and cook until the liquid evaporated each time, mixing often. Repeat this process until all but 1 ladle is absorbed. Add the asparagus and a little more salt and pepper along with the last ladle of broth, mix in, and cook until the liquid is absorbed. Add the peas and spinach, mix, and cook for about a minute. Add the steak and cream, mix, and cook for another minute. Remove from the heat, check for seasoning, and add 1 tablespoon of butter, the cheese, and fresh parsley. Serve immediately.

Turkey Chili

1½ lb ground turkey

½ lb ground beef

1 cup white wine, room temperature

1 cup chicken broth, warm

1 large red onion, diced

6 garlic cloves, minced

3 large jalapenos, seeds removed and diced

1 large green bell pepper, seeds removed, quartered
    and sliced

1 can white cannellini beans, drained

1 can black beans, drained

1 cup fresh corn kernels

2 14.5 oz cans tomato sauce

2 tbsp tomato paste

½ tbsp cumin

2 tbsp dried parsley

1 tbsp dried oregano

½ tbsp granulated garlic

½ tsp cayenne pepper

1 cup chopped fresh spinach

1 cup chopped fresh parsley

Freshly grated pecorino Romano cheese

NOTES

NOTES

Heat 2 tablespoons of olive oil in a large Dutch oven over medium-high heat. Add the ground beef and ground turkey, season with salt and pepper, and cook until it is starting to brown. Add the onions, jalapenos, and green bell peppers, and cook together until the vegetables start to soften. Add the garlic, and cook for another minute. Add the white wine, cumin, dried herbs, and granulated garlic; bring to a boil, reduce the heat, and cook until the wine is cooked down. Add the beans, tomato sauce, and tomato paste, and mix well to incorporate. Add the chicken broth, some salt and pepper and the cayenne pepper, and simmer for about 30 minutes on medium-low heat, mixing occasionally. After 30 minutes, check for seasoning, add the corn, spinach, and fresh parsley, and cook for about 5 minutes. Serve hot with some grated pecorino Romano cheese.

American, Born Overseas: The Future Is Ahead

None of us knows what the future holds, but looking back at my past, I realize it has been a wonderful adventure. All things good and bad, and everything I've learned so far, have made me into the person I am today. Looking to my future, I pray the adventure will continue, and even though I know there will be hardships, I also know there will be joy and God will continue to guide me and teach me as I go. Cooking is now a part of me that cannot be removed, and I hope to continue being as excited about it as I have been so far. I treasure my humble beginnings and my Romanian roots because without them the rest of my life wouldn't have been what it is. As the future unfolds, I look forward to more cooking, new recipes, learning more things, and becoming better. I look forward to continuing to develop my relationship with God, enriching my marriage, watching my children grow, becoming closer to my friends, and making new ones. My desire is to stay teachable and realize that no matter how much we all grow in wisdom and understanding, there is always something new we can learn! I am grateful for my whole life, and I want to say to all of you that your adventure is waiting around the corner and the dream that you have can be realized!

SECTION 3

I Love the Holidays:
Easter, Thanksgiving, and Christmas

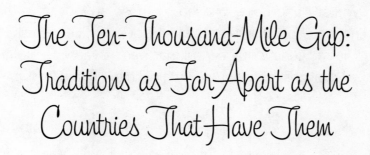

The Ten-Thousand-Mile Gap: Traditions as Far Apart as the Countries That Have Them

Holidays are quite different in Romania than they are here in the states. For one thing, Romania doesn't have the Thanksgiving holiday. They have Easter and Christmas, and what they eat is quite different than what Americans eat. There is no Easter egg hunt, and the food staple is lamb, roasted in the oven with green onions and green garlic. No mint jelly! For Christmas, it is mostly pork, cooked in a variety of ways, accompanied by side dishes made with potatoes, beans, and rice, and also a very traditional dish, which is cabbage rolls stuffed with pork and rice and served with a sort of cabbage stew. It is called *Sarmale cu varza*, which literally means, "Stuffed cabbage rolls with cabbage." The food is good, the wine is flowing, and the celebrations for both holidays usually last into the wee hours of the night! Well, at least in my family they did. We didn't have buffet-style gatherings. We had long tables covered with white linen cloths, the "good" china and silverware, which came out only on special occasions, and a meal that started about one or two in the afternoon and ended past midnight. All this time most of the guests sat down, ate, drank, and had a great time while the hostess was usually dehydrated and dead on her feet by the end because all she did was serve, wipe spills, schlep empty dishes, and constantly bring fresh food! I know, it sounds mean, but it really was tradition, and the other women at the gathering would sometimes help. We all did it whenever our turn came, and even though it was exhausting, it was also fulfilling. A sense of accomplishment came with having done all the cooking and the serving and even the cleaning yourself and being praised by those at your table for the tasty food, beautiful table setting, and considerable stamina! Obviously, I can't talk for every family in the country as to their traditions, but the food that was served was pretty much the same everywhere, and the traditions I mentioned were definitely in my family!

My Turn to Be Exhausted: My First Holiday Dinner Party

The first holiday I hosted as a married woman was Easter! My husband and I got married in December, and we celebrated Christmas at his father's house. But I wanted to do my own, so I chose Easter because it was the one that was coming next. My parents were in Romania, but I was very close to a couple that basically took me under their wings right after I came to America. They were Christians who actually walked the Christian walk and not just talked the Christian talk. They were there for me when I took my first uncertain steps in a world completely different from my own, and they were there to guide me in the beginning of my Christian walk! So they stood for me at my wedding as my parents. They were the ones I invited along with my in-laws for my first important dinner party as a new wife! No pressure! I made oven-roasted leg of lamb, a boiled potato dish, and a refreshing beef-and-lamb bone soup for the next day. There were other side dishes, but it's been twelve years, and I honestly don't remember what they were because I didn't start writing down my recipes until much later! My in-laws actually lived in a different town, so they stayed overnight, which meant I had to cover the next day as well! It was a lot of work, especially since still being new to this country I didn't know you could actually buy a deboned leg of lamb! So I bought a mammoth one, bone in, and deboned it myself. Fun!

Laura Laird

In the end, though, I was happy I went to all the trouble because everyone was impressed, and my first major dinner party as a new wife was a success! Here are two recipes from that diner party.

Oven-Roasted Leg of Lamb

1 boneless leg of lamb

12 to 14 medium to small garlic cloves, peeled and
slightly crushed

1 package-salted pork cut in small pieces, about ½
inch by 1 inch

½ cup good olive oil

¼ cup balsamic vinegar

¼ cup good red wine

6 garlic cloves, minced

½ cup minced fresh parsley

2 tbsp dried oregano

½ tsp cayenne pepper

1 bunch parsley

¼ cup fresh basil

6 garlic cloves

3 tbsp olive oil

Salt and pepper

Add ingredients 4 through 10 along with salt and pepper to taste to a jar fitted with a tight lid. Shake well to combine. Take the lamb out of the package, and allow it to open on a large cutting board. Trim any excess fat, and start cutting the lamb a little at the time in the places where it's gathered together until it is one fairly flat piece. With the tip

NOTES

of a small, sharp paring knife, start making small cuts into the lamb everywhere the meat is thick. The cuts should be about ¾ to 1 inch deep but only about ½ an inch wide. Take one crushed garlic clove and one piece of the salted pork and insert them deep into each whole. Place the lamb, inside facing up, into a deep dish, and pour some of the marinade from the jar all over. Fold the lamb in 2, pour some of the marinade on one side, turn, and pour the rest of the marinade all over. Cover the dish tightly with plastic wrap, and place it in the refrigerator for at least 4 hours or overnight. Preheat the oven to 400 degrees. Take the lamb out of the dish, pat dry with paper towels, and set aside. Pour the marinade in a small saucepan, bring to a boil, and let it simmer for a few minutes. Remove from the heat, and let it cool. Open the lamb, inside facing up, and season with salt and pepper. In a small food processor, combine ingredients 11 through 14, and process until they form a paste. Season with salt and pepper, and spread the paste all over the inside of the lamb. Close the lamb, and tie it with kitchen string. Season the whole thing with salt and pepper, and place it in a roasting pan fitted with a rack. Let the pan sit at room temperature for 10 to 15 minutes. After that time, pour a few tablespoons of the boiled marinade over the lamb, place the pan in the preheated 400-degree oven, and roast for about 15 to 20 minutes per pound until the inside temperature reaches 145 degrees for medium rare. Baste the lamb with more of the marinade 2 more times during the cooking process. When the lamb is done, take the pan out of the oven, cover tightly with aluminum foil and let it rest about 15 minutes before carving.

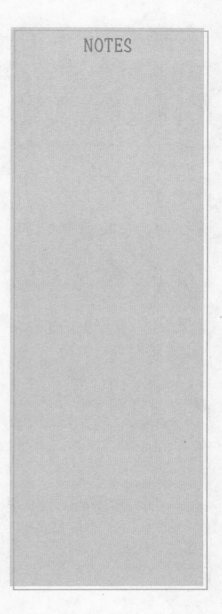

NOTES

NOTES

Chunky Potatoes with Dill and Parsley

1 lb small red potatoes cut in half
1 cup or more chicken stock, warm
1 small red onion, finely diced
6 cloves of garlic, minced
2 tbsp cream, warm
1 cup chopped fresh dill and parsley
Olive oil
Butter
¼ tsp cayenne pepper
Salt and pepper

Place the potatoes in a pan, and cover with cold water. Bring to a boil, and continue boiling for about 10 minutes until they are starting to soften but they are not cooked through. Drain the potatoes well. In a large saucepan, heat 3 tablespoons of butter and 2 tablespoons of olive oil until hot. Add the onion, and cook until translucent, mixing often. Add the garlic, and cook for one minute. Add the potatoes, season with salt and pepper, and mix well. Cook the potatoes until they start to brown, mixing well. Add the warm chicken broth, enough to come midway to the potatoes, the cayenne pepper; mix, cover, and cook until the broth evaporates. Uncover, add the cream and the fresh herbs, mix well, and cook for an additional 3 to 5 minutes.

Now That's One Big Bird

One of the things about Thanksgiving and Christmas is that they can get a little predictable when it comes to food! Turkey is a huge staple in American holiday cooking, and it is probably not a good idea to deviate too much or not use it at all. But one year when the family gathered at our house for Christmas, I really wanted to do something different! So I started thinking and researching, and I came across something very interesting, to say the least. Have you ever heard of turducken? If you haven't, don't worry. I hadn't either until that Christmas! Basically, turducken is a small, deboned chicken, stuffed inside a larger de-boned duck, stuffed inside a semi-deboned, very large turkey. Usually stuffing is placed in the chicken and/or in between all the birds. The result is a gigantic creation that takes at least 12 hours to prepare. It's like the bird equivalents of Arnold Schwarzenegger, Dwayne "The Rock" Johnson, and Oscar De La Hoya got together and decided to morph into one entity who could potentially bring down the entire bird world! What I'm saying is this is one gigantic bird! Also, it is my opinion that one would have to be quite an accomplished chef to pull this off. I'm good, but I'm not that good, not to mention I didn't really have 12 to 16 hours to dedicate to this one dish. But I wanted to make it, or at least make something like it. So I came up with the idea of making a roulade. Basically I rolled together turkey, chicken, and duck with a really good dressing in between. It still took some time, but not 12 hours, and the result was something everyone loved! Here's that recipe for your enjoyment:

NOTES

Turducken Roulade

1 6 to 7 lbs turkey breast, cut in half and each piece
   pounded to about 1/2 inch or less thickness
6 chicken breast halves, pounded thin
2 duck breasts, skin and fat removed, sliced in 6 slices
   each
2 pkgs bacon
1 lg red onion, chopped
2 med leeks, white and light green part only, chopped
1 lg shallot, chopped
6 to 8 garlic cloves, minced
½ lb mini portabella (crimini) mushrooms, sliced
1½ cups baby spinach leaves, julienned
1 cup pitted Kalamata olives, chopped
½ cup dried cranberries, chopped
1½ cups Italian style panko breadcrumbs
2/3 cup white wine
Olive oil
Butter
Salt and pepper
Cayenne pepper

Preheat oven to 350 degrees.

In a large sauté pan, heat 1 tablespoon of butter and 2 tablespoons of olive oil on medium-high until hot but not smoking. Add the mushrooms and cook until browned. After they are cooked, add salt to taste, cook for another minute, and then remove and set aside. To the same pan, add 2 tablespoons of olive oil; then add the onions, leeks, and shallots. Cook until softened but not mushy. Add the mushrooms back in the pan; then add the olives and cranberries. Cook together for a few minutes; then add the wine and the breadcrumbs. Cook until the breadcrumbs are well incorporated and the wine is almost all absorbed. Add the spinach; season with salt, pepper, and cayenne pepper to taste and cook together until the wine is completely absorbed and the mixture has the consistency of stuffing. Remove from heat, and set aside to cool. On a large work surface, place a large piece of aluminum foil and then place one of the pounded turkey breast halves on top. Season the meat with salt and pepper, then spread some of the stuffing mixture all over the meat, leaving about an inch margin all around. Place 3 of the pounded chicken halves on top of the stuffing, season with salt, and then spread more stuffing mixture. Place 6 of the duck breast slices in the middle of the turkey breast long ways. From the smaller side start rolling the turducken, tucking in as you go until it forms a roulade. Using kitchen twine, tie the roulade in several places so that it is secure. On

NOTES

223

NOTES

a large piece of parchment paper, layer the bacon slices long ways, slightly overlapping them, enough pieces to cover the whole length of the roulade. Place the roulade on top on the bacon, and roll the roulade until it is covered in the bacon pieces. You can use the parchment paper to help roll the meat. Roll the whole thing in the parchment paper, tuck in the ends, and then roll again in a large enough piece of aluminum foil to cover the entire roulade. Close the ends. Repeat for the second turkey breast half. If cooking only one roulade, bake in a roasting pan on a rack until the temperature reaches 150 to 155 degrees, for about 1 to 1 and ½ hours. For both roulades, cook for about 2½ to 3 hours or until they each reach the same temperature of 150 to 155 degrees. About 15 minutes before the roulade finishes cooking, take it from the oven, remove the aluminum foil and parchment paper, place it back in the oven, and continue cooking. This will allow the bacon to crisp up. Enjoy!

Gobble, Gobble, Gobble, Turkey Is King

Since both Thanksgiving and Christmas claim the turkey as the go-to main dish, here's a roast turkey recipe that can be used anytime! Different herbs can be used for taste variations.

Garlic Sage-Butter Roast Turkey

Note: Allow about 12 to 14 minutes per lb cooking time at 325 degrees.

NOTES

1 large turkey, room temperature, giblets removed

1 stick butter, room temperature

2 tbsp minced fresh sage

6 to 8 fresh sage leaves

1 small bunch fresh sage

4 large garlic cloves, grated

½ yellow onion cut in half

1 head of garlic cut in half crosswise

1 small red bell pepper quartered

Olive oil

Salt and pepper

Preheat oven to 325 degrees. Pat the turkey dry inside and out with paper towels. In a bowl, add the softened butter, minced sage, grated garlic, 2 teaspoons of salt, and 1

NOTES

teaspoon of pepper, and mix together until well incorporated. Season the cavity of the turkey generously with salt and pepper, and place the turkey on the rack in a large roasting pan. Place the onion halves, red bell pepper quarters, garlic halves, and the bunch of fresh sage inside the cavity. Using your fingers, very gently start loosening the skin from the turkey breast, making sure not to penetrate the skin. Divide the butter and sage mixture in two parts, and start rubbing the turkey breast under the skin with half of the mixture, distributing the butter evenly over the whole breast. Place the sage leaves over the butter under the skin. Replace the skin, wash your hands, and generously season the outside of the turkey with salt and pepper. Add 2 tablespoons of olive oil to the other half of the sage butter mixture, and mix to incorporate. Using your fingers again, start rubbing the butter, sage, and olive oil mixture all over the outside of the turkey. For the rubbing inside and out to work properly, the turkey has to be at room temperature. Season the whole turkey again lightly with some salt and pepper. Using kitchen string, tie the turkey legs together tightly and tuck the wing tips under the body. Roast the turkey in the preheated oven for about 12 to 14 minutes per pound until an instant thermometer inserted in the center of the breast reads 160 degrees. Check the turkey about midway through the cooking process, and cover the breast lightly with some aluminum foil if the skin is starting to brown too much. The butter on the breast under the skin and all over the outside of the turkey will baste and flavor the turkey so there is no need for basting throughout the cooking. Remove the turkey from the oven when done, cover loosely with aluminum foil, and let it rest at least 15 minutes before carving.

NOTES

Carving tip from the author:

The best way to keep meat moist is to cut it against the grain. In order to achieve that with the turkey breast, try removing each breast half from the bone and cutting it against the grain, a little slanted, starting at the thick end.

'Tis the Season: Smaller Gatherings during the Holidays

Christmas day is not the only time most of us entertain during the holidays. We all invite friends and family for dinner and gift exchanging all throughout the Christmas season, and many times those gatherings have a smaller amount of people. What we serve is usually different than the "big day" menu as well, but we still want to make rich, delicious foods that remind us we are in a time of celebration. Here are some recipe ideas for those kinds of smaller dinner parties.

Marinated Roasted Whole Duck

1 4 to 5 ½ lb whole duck
2 shallots, peeled and halved
½ lemon, halved
2 sprigs basil
½ cup olive oil
¼ cup lemon juice
1 tsp lemon zest
2 tbsp balsamic vinegar
1 tbsp dried basil
2 tbsp dried parsley
1 tsp paprika
½ tsp cayenne pepper
Salt and pepper

Place ingredients 5 through 12 and some salt and pepper to taste in a jar fitted with a tight lid and shake until well incorporated. Place the whole duck in a large Ziploc bag, and pour the marinade over the duck. Close the bag tightly, and move the duck around in the marinade. Place the bag inside a shallow pan, and refrigerate for at least 6 hours. Move the duck around in the marinade again at least once more. Preheat the oven to 375 degrees. Take the duck out of the marinade, and pat it dry with paper towels on the outside and inside the cavity. Allow the duck to sit at room temperature for at least 20 minutes before roasting. Bring the marinade to a boil in a small saucepan, and continue to boil it gently for about 5 to 7 minutes. Set aside to cool. Line the bottom of a large roasting pan fitted with a roasting rack with aluminum paper. Season the duck liberally with salt and pepper inside and out. Place the shallots, basil sprigs, and lemon halves inside the duck cavity, slightly cross the legs, and tie the ends with kitchen string. Place the roasting rack inside the roasting pan and the duck on the roasting rack. Tuck the wing tips under the body, and roast the duck in the preheated 375-degree oven for about 20 to 22 minutes per pound or until the internal temperature at the leg joint reaches 175 to 180 degrees and the juices run clear. Baste the duck 2 times during the cooking process with the boiled marinade. When done, take the duck out of the oven, cover it loosely with aluminum foil, and let it rest for about 15 minutes before carving.

NOTES

NOTES

Roasted Cornish Hens with a Thyme-Pomegranate-Sour Cream Glaze

2 Cornish hens, about 2 lb each
2 tbsp olive oil
¼ cup pomegranate juice
½ cup sour cream
2 tbsp minced fresh thyme
Zest of 1 lemon
Juice of ½ lemon
Salt and pepper

Preheat oven to 375 degrees. Add the olive oil, pomegranate juice, sour cream, thyme, lemon juice and zest, and some salt and pepper to a bowl, and mix well to incorporate. Place one hen on a cutting board, breast side down, and using kitchen sheers, very carefully cut down the back of the hen along one side of the spine bone from top to bottom. Do the same on the other side, and remove the spine bone along with the neck. Repeat for the second hen, and discard the spine bones or freeze and use later to make stock. Pat each hen dry with paper towels and season with salt and pepper inside and out. Place the hens on a rack set inside a large sheet pan, skin side up, and using a large kitchen brush, slather each hen with some of the glaze. Roast in the preheated oven for about 45 minutes or until an instant thermometer inserted in the thickest part of the thigh reads 160 degrees. About halfway through the cooking process, brush the hens one more time with the glaze.

NOTES

NOTES

To me, the best accompaniment for the hens is dirty spicy brown rice and chayote squash sautéed in a white wine, lemon cream sauce. Here are the recipes:

Dirty Spicy Brown Rice

1½ cups brown rice

½ cup white wine, room temperature

3½ cups beef broth, warm

4 celery stocks, halved lengthwise then sliced

3 small jalapeno pepper, seeds and veins removed and finely chopped

1 yellow onion, finely diced

6 large garlic cloves, minced

4 fresh spicy Italian sausages, skin removed and broken in small pieces

2 tbsp dried parsley

2 tbsp dried dill

½ tsp cayenne pepper

½ cup chopped spinach

1 cup chopped fresh parsley

¼ cup cream, warm

Olive oil

Butter

Salt and pepper to taste

Place a large saucepan on medium-high heat, and add 2 tablespoons of butter and 2 tablespoons of olive oil. When hot, add the onion, celery, and jalapeno peppers, and sauté until slightly softened. Add the sausage, and cook for about 5 minutes, mixing often. Add the wine, and cook until the liquid is evaporated. Add the rice, and sauté together for a couple of minutes. Add the warm beef broth, dried herbs, cayenne pepper, and salt and pepper to taste; mix and bring to a boil. Turn the heat down to low, cover, and simmer for about 40 to 45 minutes until the liquid is absorbed and the rice is cooked. Right before the rice is done, add the cream and spinach; mix and finish cooking. When done, remove from the heat, fluff with a fork, add 1 tablespoon of butter and the fresh spinach; mix in gently with the fork, check for seasoning, and serve.

NOTES

Chayote Squash with Wine, Lemon Cream Sauce

4 medium chayote squash, peeled and cut in half
1 cup white wine, room temperature
½ cup cream
¼ cup fresh lemon juice
½ cup + 2 tbsp minced fresh parsley
Butter
Salt and pepper

Cut each squash half in half again, and gently remove the pit with a paring knife. Cut each quarter in half, and set aside. You should have 32 pieces total. Place a large sauté pan on medium-high heat and add 4 tablespoons of butter. When melted, add the squash and sauté until it is starting to brown, mixing often. Add the wine, season with salt and pepper, and cook until the wine is evaporated. Add the cream, and cook until the sauce is thickened and it coats the back of a wooden spoon. Add the lemon juice, mix, remove from the heat, and check for seasoning. Mix in ½ a cup of parsley, and serve hot, sprinkled with some fresh parsley.

Citrus-Marinated Roasted Quail with Basil Cream Sauce

8 whole quail (2 per person)

3 tbsp lemon juice

¼ cup orange juice

1 tbsp minced fresh basil

1 tbsp minced fresh parsley

2 large shallots, halved and thinly sliced

8 large fresh basil leaves, chopped

1 cup white wine

½ cup cream, warm

½ tbsp lemon juice

Olive oil

Butter

Salt and pepper

Season the quail with salt and pepper inside and out, and place them in a large plastic or glass shallow dish. Mix the lemon and orange juice, and pour over the quail. Cover with plastic wrap, and refrigerate for at least 4 hours. Preheat oven to 375 degrees. Take the quail out of the refrigerator, and allow to sit at room temperature for at least 20 minutes. In the meantime, mix 6 tablespoons of olive oil and some salt and pepper with the minced parsley and basil. Season the quail with salt and pepper, and

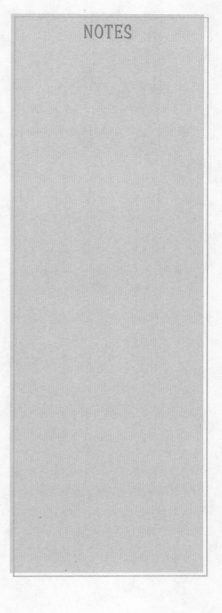

NOTES

237

NOTES

rub them all over with the olive oil mixture. Tie the legs of each quail with kitchen string and roast in the preheated 375-degree oven for about 20 minutes. In the meantime, add 1 tablespoon of butter and 1 tablespoon of olive oil to a medium saucepan set on medium heat. Add the shallots, and sauté until translucent. Add the chopped basil leaves, season with salt and pepper, and sauté for about a minute. Add the white wine, and simmer until the liquid reduces by half. Add the cream, and simmer until the sauce coats the back of a wooden spoon. Remove from the heat, add 1 tablespoon of softened butter, and gently whisk the sauce until the butter is dissolved. Check for seasoning, gently whisk in ½ a tablespoon of lemon juice, and set aside, covered. When the quail are done, remove from the oven and let them rest a few minutes. Serve with the basil cream sauce.

Christmas Pork Roulade

½ cup olive oil

¼ cup balsamic vinegar

2 tbsp red wine

2 tbsp coarsely chopped fresh parsley

2 tbsp coarsely chopped fresh dill

Salt and Pepper

3 boneless pork loin chops, about 2 inches thick

6 white cap mushrooms, peeled and sliced thin

1 large red bell pepper, quartered and sliced thin

1 large green bell pepper, quartered and sliced thin

1 large yellow bell pepper, quartered and sliced thin

Olive oil

Butter

Salt and pepper to taste

Preheat oven to 375 degrees. Add the first 5 ingredients and some salt and pepper to a jar fitted with a tight lid. Close the lid tight, and shake well to incorporate. Set aside. Cut each pork loin in half, crosswise in two 1-inch thick pieces. Pound each piece until it is about double in size and about ¼ inch thick. Try not to rip the meat while pounding it. Season each piece with salt and pepper. Start layering each piece into a large, shallow dish, pouring some of the marinade over each piece. After you layered the last piece, pour any left over marinade over all the pieces. Cover the dish with plastic wrap, and set aside. In a large sauté pan, heat 3 tablespoons of butter and 1 tablespoon of olive oil until hot. Add the sliced mushrooms and bell peppers, season with salt and pepper, and cook until slightly softened. The vegetables should be tender but still al dente and keeping their bright color since they will finish cooking in the oven. Start assembling the roulades by placing each pounded pork loin slice on a cutting board and patting it dry with some paper towel. Divide the vegetable mixture in 6 equal parts, and start rolling the meat and vegetable mixture together until it forms a long roll. Tie each roll with some kitchen string in 3 or 4 places, not too tight but tight enough to hold and season with salt and pepper. Place an ovenproof sauté pan large enough to fit all 6 rolls on medium-high heat and add 3 tablespoons of butter. When hot, sear the rolls for about 3 minutes, turning often to brown each side. Place the pan in the preheated oven, and cook for an additional 15 minutes. When ready, remove from the oven and allow the rolls to cool for about 5 to 7 minutes. Gently trim the ends of each roll, remove the strings, and cut each roll in half. Allow 3 halves per person, and serve by arranging the rolls in the middle of the plate, cut side facing up over some seasoned rice, cheesy mashed potatoes, or even a crisp salad. Besides being very tasty, this is also a very beautiful and festive dish.

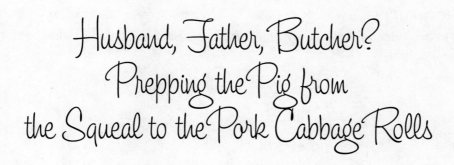

Husband, Father, Butcher? Prepping the Pig from the Squeal to the Pork Cabbage Rolls

As I mentioned earlier, in my family, pork was the staple meat for the Christmas holidays. So in the years when my fraternal grandparents raised the pig, the whole family was involved when it came time for the animal to play its most important role. So my parents and I and my father's sister, her husband, and her daughter stayed at my grandparent's house for a few days before Christmas day. On Christmas Eve morning, my father, uncle, and grandfather would wake up very early in the morning, usually before the sun was all the way up, and, despite the bitter cold and snow, they would start with the first and most unpleasant task. My cousin and I were not allowed to watch, of course, but no one could stop us from hearing what was going on. After a quick initial cleaning of the pig and the "crime scene," my mother, aunt, and grandmother would join the party for cutting and cleaning of the different cuts of meat and the inside of the pig. While we were still little girls, my cousin and I got to go out late in the morning, play in the snow, and reap the rewards of someone else's work, but when we grew up some, we became part of the work team. None of the things we had to do before the actual cooking were particularly pleasant

Laura Laird

things to do, but they had to be done! It took hours of work, sometimes all day, but by the end of it all, there were slabs of bacon hanging in the cellar, different cuts of meat in the freezer, sausages on an outside line drying, and plenty of fresh food to eat! One year I remember my grandparents raised two pigs! That was quite interesting, but because they were two, a lot of people in the whole family got to have fresh pork that year! One of the most popular dishes made with pork meat by just about everyone I knew in my land were the cabbage rolls and cabbage stew. Here's my version of that delicious recipe as homage to Christmas in my land.

Pork Cabbage Rolls with Cabbage Stew

2 ½ lb ground pork

1 medium-sized green cabbage, core removed, quartered and sliced thin

2 cups white wine, room temperature

1 56 oz jar pickled cabbage leaves

2 eggs, beaten

2 large yellow onions, diced

2 large leeks, white and light-green parts only, halved then thinly sliced

6 large garlic cloves, minced

2 tbsp tomato paste, thinned with 2 tbsp cream

½ cup minced fresh dill

½ cup minced fresh parsley

1 tbsp allspice

1 lb smoked thick cut bacon, sliced

Chicken broth, warm

2 14.5 oz can tomato sauce

Olive oil

Butter

Salt and pepper

Preheat oven to 450 degrees. In a large sauté pan, heat 2 tablespoons of butter and 1 tablespoon of olive oil until hot. Add the onion and leek, and sauté until translucent. Sea-

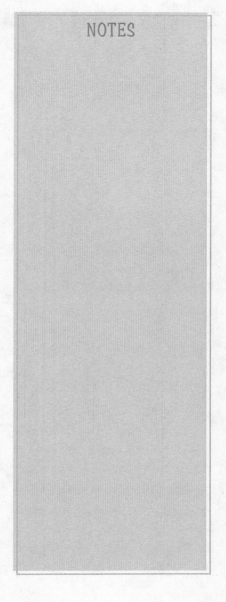

NOTES

Laura Laird

NOTES

son with salt and pepper, add the minced garlic, and sauté for another minute. Remove the onion mixture from the pan, and set aside to cool. In the same pan, add another 2 tablespoons of butter and 2 tablespoons of olive oil, and sauté the sliced cabbage on medium-high heat until it is starting to brown, mixing often. Season with salt and pepper, add 1 cup of white wine, and cook until the liquid has evaporated. Remove from heat, and set aside. Add the ground pork, onion, leek, and garlic mixture, eggs, ½ cup minced fresh dill, 1 tablespoon of allspice, 1 cup of white wine, ¼ cup olive oil, the thinned tomato paste, and salt and pepper to a very large bowl. Mix all the ingredients well, but do not overwork the meat. Chop about 1 pound of the pickled cabbage leaves, and mix with the cooled sautéed cabbage and ½ cup minced fresh parsley. Start making the cabbage rolls by placing a handful, about 2 tablespoons, of the pork mixture on the bottom of a pickled cabbage leaf, rolling it and tucking in the ends. Repeat that process until all the pork mixture is used. Place a third of the sautéed cabbage and chopped pickled cabbage mixture on the bottom of a large Dutch oven. Start arranging the cabbage rolls on top of the cabbage mixture in a circular pattern. Put some of the chopped, thick, sliced bacon on top of the cabbage rolls. Place another third of the cabbage mixture over the bacon then arrange more of the cabbage rolls in a circular pattern. Top with some more bacon, and finish with the last of the cabbage mixture. Pour the tomato sauce over the top of the cabbage rolls, and shake gently to distribute well. Add warm chicken broth to the Dutch oven until the rolls are just about covered. Place in the preheated 450-degree oven, and cook for 15 to 20 minutes. Reduce the heat down to 325 degrees, and continue cooking for 2 to 2½ hours or until an instant thermometer inserted in one of the cabbage rolls reads 160 degrees. Remove from the oven, cover the rolls, and let the rest for 10 to 15 minutes. Serve with polenta and sour cream.

NOTES

Make It Easy, Please! A Few Holiday and Yearlong Tips to Make It Easier on Yourself

Even though there are certain holiday food staples that just about everyone uses, I believe there are also dishes that are as many and as versatile as the people who make them. For me that is always a statement to the abundance this country has to offer. I am reminded as often as I go to a grocery store of the difference between the life I lived in Romania before the Revolution and the life I live here now. I hope it will always be a source of gratefulness for me, a way of keeping me grounded to the blessings in my life rather than being focused on things I might be missing. Holidays especially are joyful and fun, and I think we all miss them when they are gone and wait expectantly for them to come again! But stress can set in at holiday time as well, especially when it comes to what to make and whether or not there will be enough time. Over the years, I learned a few tricks to help me be prepared and make it easier on myself, at holiday time and all year long. I want to share some of those tips with you.

♥ If you can get a great deal on a turkey, buy an additional one to use next year! A turkey will keep a long time in the freezer, but it should probably be used within a year in order to ensure quality. Make sure to wrap it well!

♥ Buy meat and poultry in bulk at a discount retailer like Sam's or Costco, and separate it in small portions placed in freezer bags. For example, I buy big bags of chicken breast or chicken thighs, as well as small birds like quail and Cornish hens, and make individual portions, put them in freezer bags, and label them with the type of meat and the date. This way, I know how old something is and I can rotate, placing the newer things on the bottom of my freezer drawer and older things on top for immediate use. I do the same with ground meat, steak, and lamb, and even fresh sausage.

♥ Buy potatoes and onions in bulk as well, but take them out of the bags they come in and place them in the pantry inside big, shallow containers or on a metal rack.

♥ I always have a variety of rice and pastas as well as couscous and quinoa on hand. I also stack on sun-dried tomatoes packed in olive oil and roasted red bell peppers packed in water. Usually, these items can also be found in bulk, and because they have a long enough shelf life, you can buy more at once. Same goes for canned beans, canned tomatoes, and tomato sauce.

♥ Personally, I like to smash and peel my own garlic, but that's not everyone's cup of tea, so you can buy big plastic jars of already peeled garlic at the same retailers you buy the other bulk items.

♥ Contrary to some beliefs, you can freeze mozzarella and goat cheese, but not for more than two or three months. Buy in bulk, leave the cheese in its individual wrapping, and place it in freezer bags. Defrost it in the refrigerator when you're ready to use it.

I hope that all of these recipes and tips will be helpful to you and make your holiday get-togethers better and more fun. I confess that my favorite holiday is Christmas, probably because of all the presents and colorful decorations that come with it. I actually like the American tradition a little better because here I get to enjoy having the tree up a little longer, starting at the beginning of the Christmas buzz, right after Thanksgiving. In Romania, our tradition was a little different. We did not decorate the tree until Christmas Eve because that was when Santa brought the tree, along with the gifts, and left everything on the back porch or, in our case, the balcony. We kept the tree up sometimes through March, but by then the Christmas spirit was gone, and it didn't mean that much having the tree up anymore. But no matter what they are, traditions are a wonderful way to keep a steady thread of memories alive through generations. And now that I have children of my own, it is going to be interesting and fun to see what traditions my husband and I build with them.

SECTION 4

Let's End It on a Sweet Note:
A Few Recipes for Your "Sweet Tooth"

Laura Laird

I would love to be able to bake as much as I love to cook! But I'm not a baker, and so I don't make many deserts. There are a few desserts I've learned to make growing up, but in general, I don't bake. The women in my family do, and they make wonderful cakes and pies, which I hope to learn someday. Until then, however, I couldn't finish this book without writing a few desert recipes. So here are a few of them, starting with my absolute favorite sweet recipe of all time: baklava.

Baklava with Lemon Honey Syrup

1 package phyllo sheets

1 lb unsalted butter

½ lb pecans

½ lb walnuts

1 lb shelled pistachios

1 cup brown sugar

2 tsp ground cinnamon

2 tsp ground nutmeg

1 tsp ground cloves

For the lemon honey syrup:

2 cups water

1½ cups sugar

½ cup honey

¼ cup fresh lemon juice

1 tbsp lemon curd

The peel from 1 lemon

2 cinnamon sticks

4 whole cloves

1 star anise

Preheat oven to 400 degrees. Arrange the nuts in a single layer on a large sheet pan. Toast the nuts in the preheated oven for 7 to 10 minutes until golden. Remove the nuts

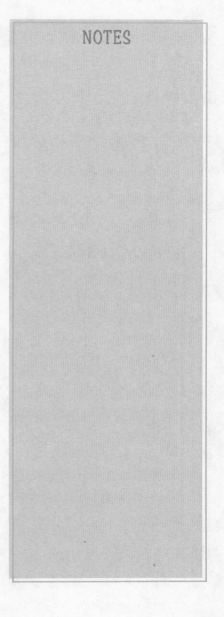

NOTES

NOTES

from the oven, and set them aside to cool. Turn the oven temperature down to 350 degrees. Wet several paper towels and squeeze dry. Cut the butter into cubes, and add them to a microwave safe dish along with 1 tablespoon of brown sugar, 1 teaspoon of ground cinnamon, 1 teaspoon of ground nutmeg, and ½ teaspoon of ground cloves, and melt on very low heat. When the nuts are cooled, chop them in a food processor, transfer them to a large bowl, and mix in the brown sugar, 1 teaspoon of ground cinnamon, 1 teaspoon of ground nutmeg, and ½ teaspoon of ground cloves. Take the phyllo sheets out of the package, and unroll them on a flat surface. Cover them with the damp paper towels. Throughout the assembling of the baklava, keep the phyllo sheets covered with damp paper towels. Brush a large sheet pan with some of the melted butter, and start by placing one phyllo sheet on the bottom. Lightly brush the phyllo sheet with some melted butter. Stack 8 to 10 phyllo sheets in this manner, one on top of each other, brushing each sheet lightly with some of the melted butter. After the last phyllo sheet, smooth gently with your hand before brushing with the butter; then add half of the nut mixture over the phyllo sheets. Smooth the mixture with the back of a wide spatula; then drizzle some of the melted butter all over the nuts. Press the mixture lightly with the spatula. Stack 4 to 6 phyllo sheets over the nut mixture, brushing each with the melted butter. Add the rest of the nut mixture on top, and proceed the same as before. Finish the baklava with 8 to 10 phyllo sheets, again brushing each with melted butter. Set the baklava aside for a few minutes to allow the butter to harden. Using a very sharp knife cut the baklava diagonally starting from the lower left corner and going across to the upper right corner in strips about 2 inches wide. Cut again in 2-inch strips starting at the upper left corner and going across to the lower right corner to form diamonds. Bake in the preheated oven for 35 to 45 minutes until golden brown. In the meantime, start making the syrup by combining the honey, lemon curd, and lemon juice in a small saucepan over medium heat. Mix gently with a spoon, and add the lemon peel when the honey is starting to liquefy. Bring to a gentle boil, lower the heat, and simmer for about 5 minutes. Set the honey mixture aside, and place a larger saucepan on medium heat. Add the water and sugar, and cook until the sugar is starting to melt, mixing often. Add the honey mixture, cinnamon sticks, star anise, and cloves; reduce the heat, and simmer for about 7 to 10 minutes until the syrup starts to thicken. Remove the lemon peel, cinnamon sticks, star anise, and cloves, and set the syrup aside to cool. When the baklava is ready, carefully remove one corner, tilt the pan, and spoon out the excess butter. Pour the syrup over the baklava, and allow it to sit for at least 4 hours or overnight before serving.

NOTES

Flan

NOTES

From the author:

Flan is known as a traditional Spanish desert, however other countries have a version of it. In France, for instance, they have "crème caramel" which roughly means "caramel custard". The Romanian translation for flan is "burnt sugar cream." We made it by cooking the sugar without water in a large pan until it melted and turned a caramel color. We then swirled the pan around to coat the bottom and sides with the sugar, allowed it to cool and harden, and then filled it with the egg custard. When I came here, I found out that caramel was made by mixing sugar with water. I like the Romanian version better because it gives the flan a deeper, nuttier taste, but it is quite complicated to do without burning the sugar, so I chose to use the water.

1½ cups sugar
3 cups milk
6 eggs
¼ cup water
1 tbsp lemon juice
2 tsp vanilla
¼ tsp salt

Preheat oven to 350 degrees. Add 1 cup of sugar and the water to a medium-sized saucepan, and gently simmer over medium heat, stirring constantly until the sugar becomes an amber color and turns to liquid. Do not let the sugar brown too much or it will become bitter. Divide the melted sugar equally between 8 medium size ramekins and swirl each ramekin around so the caramel coats the bottom and sides of the ramekins. Set them aside. The sugar will harden pretty fast but it will become soft again once the flan bakes. Beat the eggs, salt and the rest of the sugar together in a large bowl until well incorporated. Mix the milk with the vanilla and lemon juice, stir to combine and start adding the milk mixture to the eggs and sugar. Continue adding the milk to the egg mixture until all the milk is mixed in. Divide the milk mixture equally between the ramekins. Place the ramekins into a large, shallow baking pan, and fill the pan with enough hot water to come about halfway up the ramekins. Place the whole thing in the preheated oven and bake until the custard sets in the middle, about 45 to 50 minutes. The flan is ready when a knife inserted in the middle comes out clean. Let the custard cool completely before serving. To serve, invert the ramekins onto dessert plates, and garnish with some lemon zest.

NOTES

Phyllo Triangles with Sweet Cheese Filling

2 cups (16 oz) cream cheese
2 cups (16 oz) ricotta cheese
2 eggs
1/4-cup breadcrumbs
1/4-cup brown sugar
1/4-cup raisins
1-tsp nutmeg
1-tsp cinnamon
Pinch of salt, about 1/4 tsp
16 sheets phyllo dough
6 tbsp butter + 1 tsp cinnamon + 1 tsp sugar melted
   together
1 tbsp-granulated sugar

Preheat oven to 350 degrees. Place ingredients 1 through 9 in a large bowl and mix together until well incorporated. Start assembling the cheese triangles same as in the spanakopita recipe. After brushing the tops with the cinnamon and sugar melted butter, sprinkle each triangle with some granulated sugar. Bake in the preheated oven for 30 to 40 minutes and you have a very good desert or morning pastry.

Yogurt Cherry Cake with Cherry-Orange glaze

For the cake:

    1 lb pitted fresh dark cherries

    3 eggs

    1½ cups all-purpose flour

    1 tbsp baking powder

    1 tsp baking soda

    ½ tsp salt

    1½ cups plain yogurt

    2 cups + 2 tbsp sugar

    6 tbsp vegetable oil

    1 tsp vanilla extract

    1 tbsp orange zest

For the glaze:

    1½ cups confectioner's sugar

    2 tbsp cherry juice

    2 tbsp orange juice

Preheat oven to 350 degrees. Spray a 9-inch round cake pan with cooking spray, and line the bottom with parchment paper. Spray the pan again, and dust with flour. Set aside. Sprinkle the cherries with 2 tablespoons of sugar,

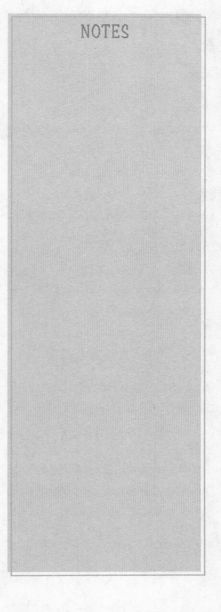

NOTES

NOTES

mix, and set aside. Sift the flour, baking powder, baking soda and salt and set aside. In a bowl, whisk together the sugar, eggs, orange zest, and vanilla until the mixture turns pale yellow and falls into ribbons. Slowly add the oil, one tablespoon at the time, and mix to incorporate. Mix in the yogurt until well incorporated. Slowly whisk in the dry ingredients. Pour the batter into the prepared cake pan, filling the pan only about ¾'s of the way up. Smooth the top with a rubber spatula. Spread the cherries evenly over the top, place the cake pan into the preheated oven, and bake for about 45 to 55 minutes until a knife inserted in the middle of the cake comes out clean. Set the cake aside to cool. In the meantime, prepare the glaze as follows: whisk together the confectioner's sugar, cherry, and orange juice until well combined. When the cake is cooled, pour the glaze over the cake and serve.

Summer Fruit Salad

2 cups quartered fresh strawberries

1½ cups sliced kiwi

1 cup canned mandarin slices, drained

2 bananas sliced

3 tbsp + a little more confectioner's sugar

1 cup plain yogurt

2 tbsp honey

½ cup orange marmalade

3 tbsp Grand Marnier orange liqueur

½ tsp freshly ground black pepper

Allow the orange marmalade to sit at room temperature for a few minutes before using. In a medium bowl, whisk together the yogurt, honey, orange marmalade, and black pepper, and set it aside at room temperature. Add all the fruit to a large plastic or glass bowl, sprinkle in the sugar, and mix gently. Add the Grand Marnier, and mix again. Allow the fruit to sit at room temperature for about 5 to 7 minutes. To serve, add some of the fruit mixture to a bowl, top with some of the flavored yogurt, and dust with a little confectioner's sugar.

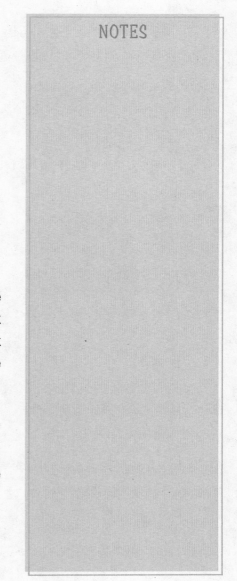

NOTES

This Is Only the Beginning: Looking Forward to the Things Ahead

Cooking means many things to many people. For me, cooking is a way of expressing myself, a way of showing love to the people around me, and it gives me a sense of accomplishment. I love everything about it, from shopping for the right ingredients to coming up with recipe ideas to serving and enjoying the finished product. Now, after writing this book, I am even more excited about cooking and learning new things in the future. But the unexpected thing that this book gave me is a realization of how grateful I am for my Romanian roots. I realize that the absence of outside ways of entertainment forced my people to create fun and excitement with what they had, and that was family and friends. And what better way to make a gathering warm and inviting than with good food prepared with love? The life I lived there may have lacked in abundance, but it was rich in time spent with my immediate and extended family and the many friends my parents and I had. I say sometimes that we might as well have had a revolving door to our apartment for the number of people that came and went all the time. Being so close sometimes created tension too, but the strong relationships we had also gave us a sense of security that no matter what we went through we always had someone there to help us. The one instance I remember most was when my father had a very serious accident which kept him away from work for a long time. I was eighteen years old, and that was a particularly hard time for my parents and me, but we were never alone. All our friends and family gathered to help in any way they could, and the emotional support that we received was priceless. I believe that kind of love and support made it easier for my parents and I to make it through that difficult time. The other side of being so close with so many people was all the fun times we had! This culture I grew up in made me who I am today, and I still love to be surrounded by people sitting at the table together, eating good food and having a great time! In fact, I thrive on those great times. I want to thank all of you for reading this book, and I hope that it will give you new ideas and a fresh love for cooking. Looking ahead to great new things, I wish you all good eating!